LUCRETIUS (c. 94–c. 55 B.C.) (3 copies)

Although he is one of Rome's greatest poets, little is known for certain about the life of Lucretius. He was probably of aristocratic birth and lived in Rome. An undocumented account appears in the CHRONICA EUSEBII of St. Jerome who states that Lucretius was driven insane by a love potion, wrote his great poem in intervals of sanity, had Cicero edit it, and at the age of forty-four committed suicide.

About the Editor

Professor Wendell Clausen, Ph.D., a graduate of the University of Washington and the University of Chicago, is currently a member of the Department of The Classics at Harvard University. Besides a number of articles in the professional journals, he has prepared editions of Persius and Juvenal, and has also supervised translated editions of Plutarch's *Lives* and Virgil's *Aeneid*. Professor Clausen is a Fellow of the American Academy in Rome.

ON THE NATURE OF THINGS

A *Washington Square Press* edition

1st printing..........................April, 1965

A new edition of a distinguished
literary work now made available in
an inexpensive, well-designed format

L

Published by
Washington Square Press, Inc., 630 Fifth Avenue, New York, N.Y.

WASHINGTON SQUARE PRESS editions are distributed in
the U.S. by Affiliated Publishers, a division of Pocket
Books, Inc., 630 Fifth Avenue, New York 20, N.Y.

ON THE NATURE
OF THINGS

Lucretius

Introduction by Wendell Clausen
Translated by H. A. J. Munro

WASHINGTON SQUARE PRESS, INC. • NEW YORK

TABLE OF CONTENTS

INTRODUCTION

Lucretius is the most solitary of Latin poets: Nothing certain is known about him except that he lived in the time of Cicero and Caesar and wrote a great poem, which he did not quite finish, *De Rerum Natura*, "On the Nature of Things." Like other sectaries of Epicurus, Lucretius must have sought inner peace, a peace he never found (to judge from his poem), by withdrawing from the world and devoting himself to the study of Epicurus' philosophy; and he all but escaped the notice of his contemporaries. Only one of them mentions him, Cicero, in a letter written in February, 54 B.C., to his brother Quintus, then serving with Caesar's army in Gaul: "The poetry of Lucretius has, as you write, many flashes of genius, yet much art." (Ancient rhetoricians tended to oppose "genius" and "art": hence the adversative form of Cicero's compliment.) There is a brief, bizarre notice of Lucretius in St. Jerome's supplements to the chronicle of Eusebius: . . . the poet Lucretius was born in 94 B.C. [or 93 or 96—the manuscripts vary]; was driven mad by a love potion; in his lucid moments wrote poetry, which Cicero later emended; and killed himself in his forty-fourth year. Despite its form, Lucretius' poem is a personal utterance, a testament—he is not, as he has been called, an impersonal poet; it discloses a passionate and melancholy man with a turbulent desire for the serenity of truth. Jerome's statement may then be factual, or in part so; or it may be little more than a biographical interpretation of certain passages in the poem: the love potion and consequent madness being suggested by the morbid, fascinated description of sexual passion at the end of Book IV, the suicide by the poet's apparent obsession especially in Book III with death.

To make Lucretius' poem intelligible, some account of Epicurus and his teaching is necessary.

Epicurus did not attain the obscurity of his illustrious disciple: Much is known about him. He was born in 342/1 B.C. of an ancient Athenian family that had fallen on hard days. About ten years before his birth his parents had gone out from Athens with other colonists to Samos, where his father farmed and kept an elementary school. When he was eighteen years old, Epicurus returned to Athens for his military training—the *ephebeia*—and then rejoined his family in Colophon, where they had sought refuge when the Athenian colonists were driven out of Samos. For several years Epicurus knew the dreary, futile existence of a refugee; and it may be in those years that he formed his main philosophical opinions. In 311/10 he opened a school in Mytilene; a little later, one in Lampsacus; his school in Lampsacus raised a sum of money and sent him to Athens, the home of philosophy. He bought a house with a walled-in garden, and there lived for about thirty-six years, devoting himself to the cultivation of his disciples, all of them his friends, and the elaboration of his philosophical opinions. And there in 271/70, after enduring a painful disease with great mildness and patience, he died.

It is significant that Epicurus sought refuge from the world in a garden; for the philosophy which he expounded there was meant to provide a refuge from the world. His disciples were of all sorts and conditions— men and women, rich and poor, slave and free: the distinctions of the world did not apply in the seclusion of the garden. No philosophy is more personal, no philosophy more obviously shaped by its inventor's experience. The conquests of Alexander (356–323 B.C.) had suddenly and drastically changed the Greek world. It was no longer a world of city-states, each separated from the others by its adjacent lands and by its own traditions and observance, in which a man might count for something: it was a world of vast empires with huge capital cities and polyglot populations, and with few traditions. How was a man to live in the midst of such an indifferent, various society? To this problem Epicurus addressed himself, and his philosophy offered an answer.

The philosophy of Epicurus is primarily concerned with ethics, or the conduct of life. Epicurus felt that man could not be happy without first ridding himself of fear, fear of the gods and fear of what might befall his soul after death. To sustain his ethical position Epicurus adopted the old atomic theory of Democritus. The universe is composed of atoms, tiny irreducible particles, and the emptiness in which they move; and of nothing else. These atoms are too small to be perceived individually by the senses; they can be perceived only in aggregation, as they combine to form the familiar things of the world: men, animals, trees, stones, dirt, water, smells, everything. The qualities of a thing—its form, density, color, temperature—vary according to the structure and kinds of its component atoms: the atoms of a stone are held together more closely than those of air, the atoms of honey are smoother and less harsh than those of wormwood. Death ensues when the structure of a thing is resolved. Once man understands the atomic structure of the world, he will no longer fear death; for he will understand that his own soul, more subtle and rare in composition but yet as temporal as all other things, will then be dispersed into its single atoms and on the instant cease to be. The gods exist—Epicurus is known to have been a pious man—but they exist out in the interstellar reaches of space, sublimely unconcerned with man and his doings, like remote potentates or perfect Epicureans.

The ethical character of Epicurus' philosophy is apparent in an innovation which he made in Democritus' system: *paregklisis*, or the doctrine of irrational atomic swerve. An infinity of atoms rains down forever through a limitless void; if these atoms fall in straight lines and at equal speeds (so Epicurus reasoned), how do they come together? At some point, at some time, for no reason, an atom swerves from its path and hits another and that hits another and that another, and from these accidents result worlds and all the things in them. This doctrine was ridiculed in antiquity—Cicero called it a "childish figment"; in recent times it has been compared favorably with the discovery that the movements of single atoms are not predictable. But Epicurus was not chiefly concerned to establish a physical fact; he was concerned to account for an ethical fact, that man has free will and can make choices of his own; and from the arbitrariness of human behavior he confidently inferred the arbitrariness of atomic behavior.

Epicureanism was as much a religion as a philosophy: The Master lived with his disciples in a kind of monastic retreat; and they venerated him, during his own lifetime, as a being more than human. To the few gathered together in his name he preached a simple, comforting gospel: The soul of man is mortal and does not survive death; the gods exist but are unmindful of us; consult your own pleasure, tranquilly and with discrimination.

Pleasure is the highest good: This Epicurus took to be self-evident, a truth of experience requiring no demonstration. No other tenet of his philosophy was so misunderstood and reviled. Epicurus did not mean that a man should snatch at any and all pleasures, however alluring; a man should first make a nice estimate of the eventual pleasure or pain involved in his choices. Some pleasures involve greater pains and are to be rejected, some pains involve greater pleasures and are to be accepted. Epicurus' own attitude was negative: the very avoidance of pain he thought pleasure. A sensual ascetic, he fervently believed that all truth was derived from experience and would not exclude even the lower pleasures of eating and drinking and sexual congress from his hedonistic calculus; but he was distrustful of sexual pleasure, feeling that most men were harmed by it, and was himself content with plain bread and water.

Epicureanism was not a poetic philosophy—the Master's own writing was notably crabbed and graceless, and he had been contemptuous of literature—but out of it Lucretius made a noble poem. Perhaps Lucretius was the first to sense the poetry in the world view of Epicurus, the first to be stirred to poetic enthusiasm by the magnificent imagined spectacle of "flaring atom-streams . . . ruining along the illimitable inane" (Tennyson, "Lucretius").

At all this a kind of godlike delight mixed with shuddering awe comes over me to think that nature by thy power is laid thus visibly open, is thus unveiled on every side.

Book III, proem

But in one way Epicureanism was a good philosophy for a poet to hold: it was a simple and sensual philosophy that proceeded from and insisted on the close observation of nature. Again and again Lucretius tells Memmius or the reader to look at the world, its myriad shapes, colors, motions; for everything in it has an exemplary significance.

... observe whenever the rays are let in and pour the
sunlight through the dark chambers of houses: you will
see many minute bodies in many ways through the
apparent void mingle in the midst of the light of the rays,
and as in never-ending conflict skirmish and give battle
combating in troops and never halting, driven about in
frequent meetings and partings; so that you may guess
from this, what it is for first-beginnings of things to be
ever tossing about in the great void.

Book II, 114–122

In Lucretius' poetry of nature there is no romantic vagueness.
In the "hues and harmonies of evening," in "clouds in starlight
widely spread" Shelley sensed mystery; Lucretius saw the
transient evidence, however beautiful, of the permanent reality that Epicurus had proclaimed to men. Of English poets
only Gerard Manley Hopkins is Lucretian in sensibility: two
poets, the one committed to a subsensual, the other to a super-
sensual reality, whose poetry nevertheless shows the keenest
delight in the world of sense; poets of passionate intelligence,
at once concrete and abstract; poets with a clear and ordered
conception of the meaning of things.

And for all this, nature is never spent;
There lives the dearest freshness deep down things;
And though the last lights off the black West went
Oh, morning, at the brown brink eastward, springs—
Because the Holy Ghost over the bent
World broods with warm breast and with ah! bright wings.

"God's Grandeur"

Hopkins' poetry alludes to—it does not expound—a detailed
system of thought. It is lyrical and not overtly didactic.

To the ancient reader a didactic poem posed no problem,
for he was used to regarding poets of all sorts as teachers;
to the modern reader, with a vague opinion that poetry should
not teach, such a poem may seen strange or perverse. He may
suppose Lucretius merely embellished an essentially prosaic
subject matter, and be tempted to read only the more "poetic"
passages, the proems or the poignant lament for mortality in

Book III. To some extent Lucretius himself is responsible for this attitude. In the proem to Book IV he seems to describe his poetry as a superficial adornment, comparing himself with the doctor who tricks children into drinking a bitter medicine by smearing the rim of the cup with honey. And the proems, the first especially, are obviously beautiful, as if Lucretius were consciously applying his own metaphor and enticing the reader onwards with a first agreeable sensation. But the reader will discover poetry as fine in the midst of the books, inextricable from the argument. True, there are inert passages of versifying as well. A poet's imagination may be engaged by a philosophy, but hardly by every tenet of it. The disadvantage of the didactic poet is this: his intellectual reach will exceed his imaginative grasp. The surprise is that Lucretius was able to transmute so much of Epicurus' philosophy into poetry and convey to the reader his own sense of wonder, delight and enthusiasm.

Lucretius meant to follow in the footsteps of his Master, for whom he felt a jealous reverence. Hercules—the type and model of the Stoic benefactor, and the two schools were at odds—Hercules traveled through the world and destroyed monsters; Epicurus in thought traveled through the universe, beyond the flaming walls of the world, and destroyed the monsters of man's own sick imagining. Books I and II of the *De Rerum Natura* deal with atomic theory: first principles, a criticism of the rival theories of Heraclitus, Empedocles, and Anaxagoras, the infinity of the universe, the motion of atoms, the formation of things, the qualities of atoms; Books III and IV with soul and mind: the nature of the soul, its mortality, the fear of death, sensation and thought, the passion of love; Books V and VI with the world: the origin of things, the evolution of man and society, celestial and terrestrial phenomena. An organized and fairly complete exposition, it would seem. But there are peculiarities: the bitter hostility to religion, which contrasts with the mild tolerance of Epicurus, and especially the obsession with death. In Book III Lucretius sets out argument after argument to prove the soul mortal; here and in the ghastly vision that closes Book VI the poet reveals himself—passionate, morbid, and despite his philosophy, not at peace.

WENDELL CLAUSEN

SELECTED BIBLIOGRAPHY

Bailey, Cyril. *Epicurus: The Extant Remains*. Oxford: Oxford University Press, 1926.

Hadzsits, George A. *Lucretius and His Influence*. New York: Longmans, Green & Co., 1935.

Hicks, Robert. *Stoic and Epicurean*. New York: (n.p.), 1910.

Murray, Gilbert. *Five Stages of Greek Religion*. Oxford: Oxford University Press, 1925. Chapters III and IV.

Santayana, George. *Three Philosophical Poets: Lucretius, Dante, and Goethe*. Cambridge, Mass.: Harvard University Press, 1910.

Book One

MOTHER of the Aeneadae, darling of men and gods, increase-giving Venus, who beneath the gliding signs of heaven fillest with thy presence the ship-carrying sea, the corn-bearing lands, since through thee every kind of living things is conceived, rises up and beholds the light of the sun. Before thee, goddess, flee the winds, the clouds of heaven; before thee and thy advent; for thee earth, manifold in works, puts forth sweet-smelling flowers; for thee the levels of the sea do laugh and heaven, propitiated, shines with outspread light. For soon as the vernal aspect of day is disclosed, and the birth-favouring breeze of Favonius unbarred is blowing fresh, first the fowls of the air, O lady, show signs of thee and thy entering in, throughly smitten in heart by thy power. Next the wild herds bound over the glad pastures and swim the rapid rivers: in such wise each, made prisoner by thy charm, follows thee with desire, whither thou goest to lead it on. Yes, throughout seas and mountains and sweeping rivers and leafy homes of birds and grassy plains, striking fond love into the breasts of all, thou constrainest them each after its kind to continue their races with desire. Since thou then art sole mistress of the nature of things, and without thee nothing rises up into the divine borders of light, nothing grows to be glad or lovely, I would have thee for a helpmate in writing the verses which I essay to pen on the nature of things for our own son of the Memmii, whom thou, goddess, hast willed to have no peer, rich as he ever is in every grace. Wherefore all the more, O lady, lend my lays an ever-living charm. Cause, meanwhile, the savage works of war to be lulled to rest throughout all seas and lands; for thou alone canst bless mankind with calm peace, seeing that Mars, lord of battle, controls the savage works of war, Mars, who often flings himself into thy lap quite vanquished by the never-healing wound of love; and then with upturned face and shapely neck thrown back feeds with love his greedy sight, gazing, goddess, open-mouthed on thee; and as backward he reclines, his breath stays hanging on thy lips. While then, lady, he is reposing on thy holy body, shed thyself about him and above, and pour from thy lips sweet discourse, asking, glorious dame, gentle peace for the Romans. For neither can we in our country's day of trouble with untroubled mind think only of our work, nor can the illustrious offset of Memmius in times like these be wanting to the general weal.

. . . for what remains to tell, apply to true reason unbusied ears and a keen mind withdrawn from cares, lest my gifts, set out for you with steadfast zeal, you abandon with disdain, before they are understood. For I will essay to discourse to you of the most high system of heaven and the gods and will open up the first-beginnings of things, out of which nature gives birth to all things and increase and nourishment, and into which nature likewise dissolves them back after their destruction. These we are accustomed, in explaining their reason, to call matter and begetting bodies of things and to name seeds of things and also to term first bodies, because from them as first elements all things are.

When human life to view lay foully prostrate upon earth crushed down under the weight of religion, who showed her head from the quarters of heaven with hideous aspect lowering upon mortals, a man of Greece ventured first to lift up his mortal eyes to her face and first to withstand her to her face. Him neither story of gods nor thunderbolts nor heaven with threatening roar could quell, but only stirred up the more the eager courage of his soul, filling him with desire to be the first to burst the fast bars of nature's portals. Therefore the living force of his soul gained the day: on he passed far beyond the flaming walls of the world and traversed throughout in mind and spirit the immeasureable universe; whence he returns a conqueror to tell us what can, what cannot come into being; in short, on what principle each thing has its powers defined, its deep-set boundary mark. Therefore religion is put under foot and trampled upon in turn; us his victory brings level with heaven.

This is what I fear herein, lest haply you should fancy that you are entering on unholy grounds of reason and treading the path of sin; whereas on the contrary often and often that heinous religion has given birth to sinful and unholy deeds. Thus in Aulis the chosen chieftains of the Danaï, foremost of men, foully polluted with Iphigenia's blood the altar of the Trivian maid. Soon as the fillet encircling her maiden tresses shed itself in equal lengths adown each cheek, and soon as she saw her father standing sorrowful before the altars and beside him the ministering priests hiding the knife and her countrymen at sight of her shedding tears, speechless in terror she dropped down on her knees and sank to the ground. Nor aught in such a moment could it avail the luckless girl that she had first bestowed the name of father on the king. For lifted up in the hands of the men, she was carried shivering to the altars, not after due performance of the customary rites to be escorted by the clear-ringing bridal song, but in the very season of marriage, stainless maid mid the stain of blood, to fall a sad victim by the sacrificing stroke of a father, that thus a happy and prosperous departure might be granted to the fleet. So great the evils to which religion could prompt!

You yourself sometime or other, overcome by the terror-speaking tales of the seers, will seek to fall away from us. Ay indeed, for how many dreams may they now imagine for you, enough to upset the calculations of life and trouble all your fortunes with fear! And with good cause; for if men saw that there was a fixed limit to their woes, they would be able in some way to withstand the religious scruples and threatenings of the seers. As it is, there is no way, no means of resisting, since they must fear after death everlasting pains. For they cannot tell what is the nature of the soul, whether it be born or on the contrary find its way into men at their birth, and whether it perish together with us when severed from us by death or visit the gloom of Orcus and wasteful pools or by divine decree find its way into brutes in our stead, as sang our Ennius, who first brought down from delightful Helicon a crown of unfading leaf, destined to bright renown throughout Italian clans of men. And yet with all this Ennius sets forth that there are Acherusian quarters, publishing it in immortal verses; though in our passage thither neither our souls nor bodies hold together, but only certain idols pale in wondrous wise. From these places he tells us the ghost of ever-living Homer uprose before him and began to shed salt tears and to unfold in words the nature of things. Wherefore we must well grasp the principle of things above, the principle by which the courses of the sun and moon go on, the force by which everything on earth proceeds, but above all we must find out by keen-sighted reason what the soul and the nature of the mind consist of, and what thing it is which meets us and frightens our minds when we are awake and under the influence of disease and when we are buried in sleep, so that we seem to see and hear speaking to us face to face them who are dead and whose bones earth holds in its embrace.

Nor does my mind fail to perceive how hard it is to make clear in Latin verses the dark discoveries of the Greeks, especially as many points must be dealt with in new terms on account of the poverty of the language and the novelty of the questions. But yet your worth and the looked-for pleasure of sweet friendship prompt me to undergo any labour and lead me on to watch the clear nights through, seeking by what words and in what verse I may be able in the end to shed on your mind so clear a light that you can thoroughly scan hidden things.

This terror then and darkness of mind must be dispelled not by the rays of the sun and glittering shafts of day, but by the aspect and the law of nature; the warp of whose design we shall begin with this first principle: nothing is ever gotten out of nothing by divine power. Fear in sooth takes such a hold of all mortals, because they see many operations go on in earth and heaven, the causes of which they can in no way understand, believing them therefore to be done by power divine. For these reasons, when we shall have seen that nothing can be produced from nothing, we shall then more correctly ascertain that which we are pursuing, both the elements out of which everything can be produced and the manner in which all things are done without the hand of the gods.

If things came from nothing, any kind might be born of anything, nothing would require seed. Men, for instance, might rise out of the sea, the scaly race out of the earth, and birds might burst out of the sky; horned and other herds, every kind of wild beasts would haunt with changing brood tilth and wilderness alike. Nor would the same fruits keep constant to trees, but would change; any tree might bear any fruit. For if there were not begetting bodies for each, how could things have a fixed, unvarying mother? But in fact, because things are all produced from fixed seeds, each thing is born and goes forth into the borders of light out of that in which resides its matter and first bodies; and for this reason all things cannot be gotten out of all things, because in particular things resides a distinct power. Again, why do we see the rose put forth in spring, corn in the season of heat, vines yielding at the call of autumn, if not because, when the fixed seeds of things have streamed together at the proper time, whatever is born discloses itself, while the due seasons are there and the quickened earth brings its weakly products in safety forth into the borders of light? But if they came from nothing, they would rise up suddenly at uncertain periods and unsuitable times of year, inasmuch as there would be no first-beginnings which might be kept from a begetting union by the unpropitious season. No, nor would time be required for the growth of things after the meeting of the seed, if they could increase out of nothing. Little babies would at once grow into men and trees in a moment would rise and start out of the ground. But none of these events, it is plain, ever comes to pass, since all things grow step by step, as is natural, [since they all grow] from a fixed seed and in growing preserve their kind; so that you may be sure that all things increase in size and are fed out of their own matter. Furthermore, without fixed seasons of rain, the earth is unable to put forth its gladdening produce, nor again, if kept from food, could the nature of living things continue its kind and sustain life; so that you might hold with greater truth that many bodies are common to many things, as we see letters common to different words, than that any thing could come into being without first-beginnings. Again, why could not nature have produced men of such a size and strength as to be able to wade on foot across the sea and rend great mountains with their hands and outlive many generations of living men, if not because an unchanging matter has been assigned for begetting things and what can arise out of this matter is fixed? We must admit therefore that nothing can come from nothing, since things require seed before they can severally be born and be brought out into the buxom fields of air. Lastly, since we see that tilled grounds surpass untilled and yield a better produce by the labour of hands, we may infer that there are in the earth first-beginnings of things which we by turning up the fruitful clods with the share and labouring the soil of the earth stimulate to rise. But if there were no such, you would see all things without any labour of ours spontaneously come forth in much greater perfection.

Moreover, nature dissolves everything back into its first bodies and does not annihilate things. For if aught were mortal in all its parts alike, the thing in a moment would be snatched away to destruction from before our eyes; since no force would be needed to produce disruption among its parts and undo their fastenings. Whereas in fact, as all things consist of an imperishable seed, nature suffers the destruction of nothing to be seen, until a force has encountered it sufficient to dash things to pieces by a blow or to pierce through the void places within them and break them up. Again, if time, whenever it makes away with things through age, utterly destroys them, eating up all their matter, out of what does Venus bring back into the light of life the race of living things each after its kind, or, when they are brought back, out of what does earth, manifold in works, give them nourishment and increase, furnishing them with food each after its kind? Out of what do its own native fountains and extraneous rivers from far and wide keep full the sea? Out of what does ether feed the stars? For infinite time gone by and lapse of days must have eaten up all things which are of mortal body. Now if in that period of time gone by those things have existed, of which this sum of things is composed and recruited, they are possessed, no doubt, of an imperishable body, and cannot therefore any of them return to nothing. Again, the same force and cause would destroy all things without distinction, unless everlasting matter held them together, matter more or less closely linked in mutual entanglement: a touch in sooth would be sufficient cause of death, inasmuch as any amount of force must of course undo the texture of things in which no parts at all were of an everlasting body. But in fact, because the fastenings of first-beginnings one with the other are unlike and matter is everlasting, things continue with body uninjured, until a force is found to encounter them strong enough to overpower the texture of each. A thing therefore never returns to nothing, but all things after disruption go back into the first bodies of matter. Lastly, rains die, when father ether has tumbled them into the lap of mother earth; but then goodly crops spring up and boughs are green with leaves upon the trees, trees themselves grow and are laden with fruit; by them in turn our race and the race of wild beasts are fed, by them we see glad towns teem with children and the leafy forests ring on all sides with the song of new birds; through them cattle, wearied with their load of fat, lay their bodies down about the glad pastures and the white milky stream pours from the distended udders; through them a new brood with weakly limbs frisks and gambols over the soft grass, their young minds smitten with the love of pure milk. None of the things therefore which seem to be lost is utterly lost, since nature replenishes one thing out of another and does not suffer anything to be begotten before she has been recruited by the death of some other.

Now mark me: since I have taught that things cannot be born from nothing, cannot when begotten be brought back to nothing, that you may not haply yet begin in any shape to mistrust my words, because the first-beginnings of things cannot be seen by the eyes, take, moreover, this list of bodies which you must yourself admit are in the number of things and cannot be seen. First of all, the force of the wind when aroused beats on the harbours and whelms huge ships and scatters clouds; sometimes in swift whirling eddy it scours the plains and straws them with large trees and scourges the mountain summits with forest-rending blasts: so fiercely does the wind rave with a shrill howling and rage with threatening roar. Winds therefore sure enough are unseen bodies which sweep the seas, the lands, ay and the clouds of heaven tormenting them and catching them up in sudden whirls. On they stream and spread destruction abroad in just the same way as the soft liquid nature of water when all at once it is borne along in an overflowing stream, and a great downfall of water from the high hills augments it with copious rains, flinging together fragments of forests and entire trees, nor can the strong bridges sustain the sudden force of coming water: in such wise, turbid with much rain, the river dashes upon the piers with mighty strength. With a loud noise the water makes havoc and rolls under its eddies huge stones and throws down whatever opposes its waves. In this way then must the blasts of wind as well move on, and when they like a mighty stream have borne down in any direction, they push things before them and throw them down with repeated assaults, sometimes catch them up in curling eddy and carry them away in swift-circling whirl. Wherefore once and again

I say winds are unseen bodies, since in their works and ways they are found to rival great rivers, which are of a visible body. Then again we perceive the different smells of things, yet never see them coming to our nostrils; nor do we behold heats nor can we observe cold with the eyes nor are we used to see voices. Yet all these things must consist of a bodily nature, since they are able to move the senses; for nothing but body can touch and be touched. Again, clothes hung up on a shore which waves break upon become moist, and then get dry if spread out in the sun. Yet it has not been seen in what way the moisture of water has sunk into them nor, again, in what way this has been dispelled by heat. The moisture therefore is dispersed into small particles which the eyes are quite unable to see. Again, after the revolution of many of the sun's years, a ring on the finger is thinned on the underside by wearing, the dripping from the eaves hollows a stone, the bent ploughshare of iron imperceptibly decreases in the fields, and we behold the stone-paved streets worn down by the feet of the multitude; the brass statues too at the gates show their right hands to be wasted by the touch of the numerous passers-by who greet them. These things then we see are lessened, since they have been thus worn down; but what bodies depart at any given time the nature of vision has jealously shut out our seeing. Lastly, the bodies which time and nature add to things by little and little, constraining them to grow in due measure, no exertion of the eyesight can behold; and so too wherever things grow old by age and decay, and when rocks hanging over the sea are eaten away by the fine salt spray, you cannot see what they lose at any given moment. Nature therefore works by unseen bodies.

And yet all things are not on all sides jammed together and kept in by body: there is also void in things. To have learned this will be good for you on many accounts; it will not suffer you to wander in doubt and to seek in the sum of things and be distrustful of our words. If there were not void, things could not move at all; for that which is the property of body, to let and hinder, would be present to all things at all times; nothing therefore could go on, since no other thing would be the first to give way. But in fact, throughout seas and lands and the heights of heaven we see before our eyes many things move in many ways for various reasons, which things, if there were no void, I need not say would lack and want restless motion: they never would have been begotten at all, since matter jammed on all sides would have been at rest. Again, however solid things are thought to be, you may yet learn from this that they are of rare body: in rocks and caverns the moisture of water oozes through and all things weep with abundant drops; food distributes itself through the whole body of living things; trees grow and yield fruit in season, because food is diffused through the whole from the very roots over the stem and all the boughs. Voices pass through walls and fly through houses shut, stiffening frost pierces to the bones. Now if there are no void parts, by what way can the bodies severally pass? You would see it to be quite impossible. Once more, why do we see one thing surpass another in weight though not larger in size? For if there is just as much body in a ball of wool as there is in a lump of lead, it is natural it should weigh the same, since the property of body is to weigh all things downwards, while on the contrary, the nature of void is ever without weight. Therefore when a thing is just as large, yet is found to be lighter, it proves sure enough that it has more of void in it; while on the other hand, that which is heavier shows that there is in it more of body and that it contains within it much less of void. Therefore that which we are seeking with keen-sighted reason exists sure enough, mixed up in things; and we call it void.

And herein I am obliged to forestall this point which some raise, lest it draw you away from the truth. The waters, they say, make way for the scaly creatures as they press on, and open liquid paths, because the fish leave room behind them, into which the yielding waters may stream; thus other things too may move and change place among themselves, although the whole sum be full. This, you are to know, has been taken up wholly on false grounds. For on what side, I ask, can the scaly creatures move forwards, unless the waters have first made room? Again, on what side can the waters give place, so long as the fish are unable to go on? Therefore you must either strip all bodies of motion or admit that in things void is mixed up from which everything gets its first start in moving. Lastly, if two broad bodies after contact quickly spring asunder, the air must surely fill all the void which is formed between the bodies, Well, however rapidly it stream together with swift-circling currents, yet the whole space will not be able to be filled up in one moment; for it must occupy first one spot and then another, until the whole is taken up. But if haply anyone supposes that, when the bodies have started asunder, that result follows because the air condenses, he is mistaken; for a void is then formed which was not before, and a void also is filled which existed before; nor can the air condense in such a way, nor supposing it could, could it methinks without void draw into itself and bring its parts together.

Wherefore however long you hold out by urging many objections, you must needs in the end admit that there is a void in things. And many more arguments I may state to you in order to accumulate proof on my words; but these slight footprints are enough for a keen-searching mind to enable you by yourself to find out all the rest. For as dogs often discover by smell the lair of a mountain-ranging wild beast though covered over with leaves, when once they have got on the sure tracks, thus you in cases like this will be able by yourself alone to see one thing after another and find your way into all dark corners and draw forth the truth. But if you lag or swerve a jot from the reality, this I can promise you, O Memmius, at once without more ado: such plenteous draughts from abundant wellsprings my sweet tongue shall pour from my richly furnished breast, that I fear slow age will steal over our limbs and break open in us the fastnesses of life, ere the whole store of reasons on any one question has by my verses been dropped into your ears.

But now to resume the thread of the design which I am weaving in verse: all nature then, as it exists by itself, has been founded on two things: there are bodies and there is void in which these bodies are placed and through which they move about. For that body exists by itself the general feeling of mankind declares; and unless the first foundation of belief shall be firmly grounded on this, there will be nothing to which we can appeal on hidden things in order to prove anything by reasoning of mind. Then again, if room and space, which we call void, did not exist, bodies could not be placed anywhere nor move about at all in any direction; as we have demonstrated to you a little before. Moreover, there is nothing which you can affirm to be at once separate from all body and quite distinct from void, which would, so to say, count as the discovery of a third nature. For whatever shall exist, this of itself must be something or other. Now if it shall admit of touch in however slight and small a measure, it will, be it with a large or be it with a little addition, provided it do exist, increase the amount of body and join the sum. But if it shall be intangible and unable to hinder anything from passing through it on any side, this, you are to know, will be that which we call empty void. Again, whatever shall exist by itself will either do something or will itself suffer by the action of other things, or else in it things will be able to exist and go on. But no thing can do and suffer without body nor aught furnish room except void and vacancy. Therefore beside void and bodies no third nature taken by itself can be left in the number of things, either such as to fall at any time under the ken of our senses or such as anyone can grasp by the reason of his mind.

For whatever things are named, you will either find to be properties linked to these two things or you will see to be accidents of these things. That is a property which can in no case be disjoined and separated without destruction accompanying the severance, such as the weight of a stone, the heat of fire, the fluidity of water. Slavery, on the other hand, poverty and riches, liberty, war, concord and all other things which may come and go while the nature of the thing remains unharmed, these we are wont, as it is right we should, to call accidents. Time also exists not by itself, but simply from the things which happen, the sense apprehends what has been done in time past, as well as what is present and what is to follow after. And we must admit that no one feels time by itself abstracted from the motion and calm rest of things. So when they say that the daughter of Tyndareus was ravished and the Trojan nations were subdued in war, we must mind that they do not force us to admit that these things are by themselves, since those generations of men, of whom these things were accidents, time now gone by has irrevocably swept away. For whatever shall have been done may be termed an accident in one case of the Teucrian people, in another of the countries simply. Yes, for if there had been no matter of things and no room and space in which things severally go on, never had the fire, kindled by love of the beauty of Tyndareus' daughter, blazed beneath the Phrygian breast of Alexander and lighted up the famous struggles of cruel war, nor had the timber horse unknown to the Trojans

wrapt Pergama in flames by its night-issuing brood of sons
of the Greeks; so that you may clearly perceive that all actions from first to last exist not by themselves and are not by
themselves in the way that body is, nor are terms of the same
kind as void is, but are rather of such a kind that you may
fairly call them accidents of body and of the room in which
they severally go on.

Bodies, again, are partly first-beginnings of things, partly
those which are formed of a union of first-beginnings. But
those which are first-beginnings of things no force can
quench: they are sure to have the better by their solid body.
Although it seems difficult to believe that aught can be found
among things with a solid body. For the lightning of heaven
passes through the walls of houses, as well as noise and
voices; iron grows red hot in the fire and rocks burning with
fierce heat burst asunder; the hardness of gold is broken up
and dissolved by heat; the ice of brass melts vanquished by
the flame; warmth and piercing cold ooze through silver,
since we have felt both, as we held cups with the hand in
due fashion and the water was poured down into them. So
universally there is found to be nothing solid in things. But
yet because true reason and the nature of things constrains,
attend until we make clear in a few verses that there are such
things as consist of solid and everlasting body, which we
teach are seeds of things and first-beginnings, out of which
the whole sum of things which now exists has been produced.

First of all, then, since there has been found to exist a twofold and widely dissimilar nature of two things, that is to say
of body and of place in which things severally go on, each of
the two must exist for and by itself and quite unmixed. For
wherever there is empty space which we call void, there body
is not; wherever, again, body maintains itself, there empty
void nowise exists. First bodies therefore are solid and without
void. Again, since there is void in things begotten, solid matter must exist about this void, and nothing can be proved by
true reason to conceal in its body and have within it void, unless you choose to allow that that which holds it in is solid.
Again, that can be nothing but a union of matter which can
keep in the void of things. Matter therefore, which consists
of a solid body, may be everlasting, though all things else are
dissolved. Moreover, if there were no empty void, the universe would be solid; unless, on the other hand, there were

certain bodies to fill up whatever places they occupied, the existing universe would be empty and void space. Therefore, sure enough, body and void are marked off in alternate layers, since the universe is neither of a perfect fullness nor a perfect void. There are therefore certain bodies capable of marking off void space from full. These can neither be broken in pieces by the stroke of blows from without nor have their texture undone by aught piercing to their core nor give way before any other kind of assault; as we have proved to you a little before. For without void nothing seems to admit of being crushed in or broken up or split in two by cutting, or of taking in wet or permeating cold or penetrating fire, by which all things are destroyed. And the more anything contains within it of void, the more thoroughly it gives way to the assault of these things. Therefore if first bodies are, as I have shown, solid and without void, they must be everlasting. Again, unless matter had been eternal, all things before this would have utterly returned to nothing and whatever things we see would have been born anew from nothing. But since I have proved above that nothing can be produced from nothing, and that what is begotten cannot be recalled to nothing, first-beginnings must be of an imperishable body, into which all things can be dissolved at their last hour, that there may be a supply of matter for the reproduction of things. Therefore first-beginnings are of solid singleness, and in no other way can they have been preserved through ages during infinite time past in order to reproduce things.

Again, if nature had set no limit to the breaking of things, by this time the bodies of matter would have been so far reduced by the breaking of past ages that nothing could within a fixed time be conceived out of them and reach its utmost growth of being. For we see that anything is more quickly destroyed than again renewed; and therefore that which the long, the infinite duration of all bygone time had broken up, demolished and destroyed could never be reproduced in all remaining time. But now, sure enough, a fixed limit to their breaking has been set, since we see each thing renewed, and at the same time definite periods fixed for things to reach the flower of their age. Moreover, while the bodies of matter are most solid, it may yet be explained in what way all things which are formed soft—as air, water, earth, fires—are so formed and by what force they severally go on, since once for

all there is void mixed up in things. But on the other hand, if
the first-beginnings of things be soft, it cannot be explained
out of what enduring basalt and iron can be produced; for
their whole nature will utterly lack a first foundation to begin
with. First-beginnings therefore are strong in solid singleness,
and by a denser combination of these all things can be closely
packed and exhibit enduring strength.

Again, if no limit has been set to the breaking of bodies,
nevertheless the several bodies which go to things must survive from eternity up to the present time, not yet assailed by
any danger. But since they are possessed of a frail nature, it
is not consistent with this that they could have continued
through eternity harassed through ages by countless blows.
Again too, since a limit of growing and sustaining life has
been assigned to things each after its kind, and since by the
laws of nature it stands decreed what they can each do and
what they cannot do, and since nothing is changed, but all
things are so constant that the different birds all in succession
exhibit in their body the distinctive marks of their kind, they
must sure enough have a body of unchangeable matter also.
For if the first-beginnings of things could in any way be vanquished and changed, it would be then uncertain too what
could and what could not rise into being, in short, on what
principle each thing has its powers defined, its deep-set
boundary mark; nor could the generations reproduce so often
each after its kind the nature, habits, way of life and motions
of the parents.

Then again, since there is ever a bounding point to that
first body which already is beyond what our senses can perceive, that point, sure enough, is without parts and consists
of a least nature and never has existed apart by itself and
will not be able in future so to exist, since it is in itself part
of that other; and so a first and single part and then other and
other similar parts in succession fill up in close serried mass
the nature of the first body; and since these cannot exist by
themselves, they must cleave to that from which they cannot
in any way be torn. First-beginnings therefore are of solid
singleness, massed together and cohering closely by means of
least parts, not compounded out of a union of those parts,
but, rather, strong in everlasting singleness. From them nature
allows nothing to be torn, nothing further to be worn away,
reserving them as seeds for things. Again, unless there shall

be at least, the very smallest bodies will consist of infinite parts, inasmuch as the half of the half will always have a half and nothing will set bounds to the division. Therefore between the sum of things and the least of things what difference will there be? There will be no distinction at all; for how absolutely infinite soever the whole sum is, yet the things which are smallest will equally consist of infinite parts. Now since on this head true reason protests and denies that the mind can believe it, you must yield and admit that there exist such things as are possessed of no parts and are of a least nature. And since these exist, those first bodies also you must admit to be solid and everlasting. Once more, if nature, creatress of things, had been wont to compel all things to be broken up into least parts, then too she would be unable to reproduce anything out of those parts, because those things which are enriched with no parts cannot have the properties which begetting matter ought to have: I mean the various entanglements, weights, blows, clashings, motions by means of which things severally go on.

For which reasons they who have held fire to be the matter of things and the sum to be formed out of fire alone, are seen to have strayed most widely from the true reason. At the head of whom enters Heraclitus to do battle, famous for obscurity more among the frivolous than the earnest Greeks who seek the truth. For fools admire and like all things the more which they perceive to be concealed under involved language, and determine things to be true which can prettily tickle the ears and are varnished over with finely sounding phrase.

For I want to know how things can be so various, if they are formed out of fire one and unmixed: it would avail nothing for hot fire to be condensed or rarefied, if the parts of fire had always the same nature which the whole fire likewise has. The heat would be more intense by compression of parts, more faint by their severance and dispersion. More than this you cannot think it in the power of such causes to effect, far less could so great a diversity of things come from mere density and rarity of fires. Observe also, if they suppose void to be mixed up in things, fire may then be condensed and left rare; but because they see many things rise up in contradiction to them and shrink from leaving unmixed void in things, fearing the steep, they lose the true road, and do not perceive on the other hand that if void is taken from things, all things are condensed and out of all things is formed one single body, which cannot briskly radiate anything from it, in the way heat-giving fire emits light and warmth, letting you see that it is not of closely compressed parts. But if they haply think that in some other way fires may be quenched in the union and change their body, you are to know that if they shall scruple on no side to do this, all heat sure enough will be utterly brought to nothing, and all things that are produced will be formed out of nothing. For whenever a thing changes and quits its proper limits, at once this change of state is the death of that which was before. Therefore something or other must needs be left to those fires of theirs undestroyed, that you may not have all things absolutely returning to nothing, and the whole store of things born anew and flourishing out of nothing. Since then in fact there are some most unquestionable bodies which always preserve the same nature, on whose going or coming and change of order things change their nature and bodies are transformed, you are to know that these first bodies of things are not of fire. For it would matter nothing that some should withdraw and go away and others should be added on and some should have their order changed, if they yet one and all retained the nature of heat; for whatever they produced would be altogether fire. But thus methinks it is: there are certain bodies whose clashings, motions, order, position, shapes produce fires, and which by a change of order change the nature of the things and do not resemble fire nor anything else which has the power of sending bodies to our senses and touching by its contact our sense of touch.

Again, to say that all things are fire and that no real thing except fire exists in the number of things, as this same man does, appears to be sheer dotage. For he himself takes his stand on the side of the senses to fight against the senses and shakes their authority, on which rests all our belief, ay, from which this fire, as he calls it, is known to himself; for he believes that the senses can truly perceive fire, he does not believe they can perceive all other things which are not a whit less clear. Now this appears to me to be as false as it is foolish; for to what shall we appeal? What surer test can we have than the senses, whereby to note truth and falsehood? Again, why should anyone rather abolish all things and choose to leave the single nature of heat, than deny that fires exist, while he allows anything else to be? It seems to be equal madness to affirm either this or that.

For these reasons, they who have held that fire is the matter of things and that the sum can be formed out of fire, and they who have determined air to be the first-beginning in begetting things, and all who have held that water by itself alone forms things, or that earth produces all things and changes into all the different natures of things, appear to have strayed exceedingly wide of the truth; as well as they who make the first-beginnings of things twofold, coupling air with fire and earth with water, and they who believe that all things grow out of four things, fire, earth and air and water. Chief of whom is Agrigentine Empedocles: him within the three-cornered shores of its lands that island bore, about which the Ionian sea flows in large cranklings, and splashes up brine from its green waves. Here the sea racing in its straitened frith divides by its waters the shores of Italia's lands from the other's coasts; here is wasteful Charybdis and here the rumblings of Etna threaten anew to gather up such fury of flames, as again with force to belch forth the fires bursting from its throat and carry up to heaven once more the lightnings of flame. Now, though this great country is seen to deserve in many ways the wonder of mankind and is held to be well worth visiting, rich in all good things, guarded by large force of men, yet seems it to have held within it nothing more glorious than this man, nothing more marvellous and dear. The verses too of his godlike genius cry with a loud voice and set forth in such wise his glorious discoveries that he hardly seems born of a mortal stock.

Yet he and those whom we have mentioned above immeasurably inferior and far beneath him, although the authors of many excellent and godlike discoveries they have given responses from, so to say, their hearts' holy of holies with more sanctity and on much more unerring grounds than the Pythia who speaks out from the tripod and laurel of Phoebus, have yet gone to ruin in the first-beginnings of things: it is there they have fallen, and, great themselves, great and heavy has been that fall; first because they have banished void from things and yet assign to them motions, and allow things soft and rare, air, sun, fire, earth, living things, corn, and yet mix not up void in their body; next because they suppose that there is no limit to the division of bodies and no stop set to their breaking and that there exists no least at all in things;

though we see that that is the bounding point of anything which seems to be least in reference to our senses, so that from this you may infer that because the things which you do not see have a bounding point, there is a least in them. Moreover, since they assign soft first-beginnings of things, which we see to have birth and to be of a body altogether mortal, both the sum of things must in that case revert to nothing and the store of things be born anew and flourish out of nothing: now how wide of the truth both of these doctrines are you will already comprehend. In the next place, these bodies are in many ways mutually hostile and poisonous; and therefore they will either perish when they have met, or will fly asunder just as we see, when a storm has gathered, lightnings and rains and winds fly asunder.

Again, if all things are produced from four things and all again broken up into those things, how can they more be called first-beginnings of things than things be called their first-beginnings, the supposition being reversed? For they are begotten time about and interchange colour and their whole nature without ceasing. But if haply you suppose that the body of fire and of earth and air and the moisture of water meet in such a way that none of them in the union changes its nature, nothing I can tell you will be able to be thus produced out of them, neither living thing nor thing with inanimate body, as a tree; in fact, each thing amid the medley of this discordant mass will display its own nature and air will be seen to be mixed up with earth and heat to remain in union with moisture. But first-beginnings ought, in begetting things, to bring with them a latent and unseen nature in order that no thing stand out, to be in the way and prevent whatever is produced from having its own proper being.

Moreover, they go back to heaven and its fires for a beginning, and first suppose that fire changes into air, next that from air water is begotten and earth is produced out of water, and that all in reverse order come back from earth, water first, next air, then heat, and that these cease not to interchange, to pass from heaven to earth, from earth to the stars of ether. All which first-beginnings must on no account do; since something unchangeable must needs remain over, that things may not utterly be brought back to nothing. For whenever a thing changes and quits its proper limits, at once this change of state is the death of that which was before. Wherefore since those things which we have mentioned a little before pass into a state of change, they must be formed out of others which cannot in any case be transformed, that you may not have things returning altogether to nothing. Why not rather hold that there are certain bodies possessed of such a nature that, if they have haply produced fire, the same may, after a few have been taken away and a few added on and the order and motion changed, produce air; and that all other things may in the same way interchange with one another?

"But plain matter of fact clearly proves," you say, "that all things grow up into the air and are fed out of the earth; and unless the season at the propitious period send such abundant showers that the trees reel beneath the soaking storms of rain, and unless the sun on its part foster them and supply heat, corn, trees, living things could not grow." Quite true, and unless solid food and soft water should recruit us, the body would waste away and then the whole life would break up out of all the sinews and bones; for we beyond doubt are recruited and fed by certain things, this and that other thing by certain other things. Because many first-beginnings common to many things in many ways are mixed up in things, therefore, sure enough, different things are fed by different things. And it often makes a great difference with what things and in what position the same first-beginnings are held in union and what motions they mutually impart and receive; for the same make up heaven, sea, lands, rivers, sun, the same make up corn, trees, living things; but they are mixed up with different things and in different ways as they move. Nay, you see throughout even in these verses of ours many elements common to many words, though you must needs admit that the lines and words differ one from the other both in meaning and in the sound wherewith they sound. So much can elements effect by a mere change of order; but those elements which are the first-beginnings of things can bring with them more combinations out of which different things can severally be produced.

Let us now also examine the homoeomeria of Anaxagoras, as the Greeks term it, which the poverty of our native speech does not allow us to name in our own tongue; though it is easy enough to set forth in words the thing itself. First of all then, when he speaks of the homoeomeria of things, you must know he supposes bones to be formed out of very small and minute bones and flesh of very small and minute fleshes and blood by the coming together of many drops of blood, and gold he thinks can be composed of grains of gold and earth be a concretion of small earths and fires can come from fires and water from waters, and everything else he fancies and supposes to be produced on a like principle. And yet at the same time he does not allow that void exists anywhere in things, or that there is a limit to the division of things. Wherefore he appears to me on both these grounds to be as much mistaken as those whom we have already spoken of above. In addition to this the first-beginnings which he supposes are too frail; if first-beginnings they be which are possessed of a nature like to the things themselves and are just as liable to suffering and death, and which nothing reins back from destruction. For which of them will hold out against a strong crushing force, so as to escape death, in the very jaws of destruction—fire or water or air? Which of these—blood or bones? Not one, methinks, since everything will be just as essentially mortal as those things which we see with the senses perish before our eyes vanquished by some force. But I appeal to facts demonstrated above for proof that things cannot fall away to nothing nor on the other hand grow from nothing. Again, since food gives increase and nourishment to the body, you are to know that our veins and blood and bones [and the like are formed of things foreign to them in kind]; or if they shall say that all foods are of a mixed body and contain in them small bodies of sinews and bones and veins as well and particles of blood, it will follow that all food, solid as well as liquid, must be held to be composed of things foreign to them in kind, of bones, that is, and sinews and matter and blood mixed up. Again, if all the bodies which grow out of the earth are in the earths, the earth must be composed of things foreign to it in kind which grow out of these earths. Apply again this reasoning to other things, and you may use just the same words. If flame and smoke and ash are latent in woods, woods must necessarily be composed of things foreign to them in kind. Again, all those bodies to which the earth gives food, it increases [out of things foreign to them in kind which rise out of the earth: thus too the bodies of flame which issue from the woods, are fed] out of things foreign to them in kind which rise out of these woods.

Here some slight opening is left for evasion, which Anaxagoras avails himself of, choosing to suppose that all things though latent are mixed up in things, and that is alone visible of which there are the largest number of bodies in the mixture and these more ready to hand and stationed in the first rank. This, however, is far banished from true reason. For then it were natural that corn too should often, when crushed by the formidable force of the stone, show some mark of blood or some other of the things which have their nourishment in our body; and when we rub one stone on another, blood should ooze out. For like reasons it were fitting that grasses too should yield sweet drops of liquid, like in flavour to the udder of milk in sheep; yes and that often, when clods of earth have been crumbled, kinds of grasses and corn and leaves should be found to lurk distributed among the earth in minute quantities; and lastly that ash and smoke and minute fires should be found latent in woods, when they were broken off. Now since plain matter of fact teaches that none of these results follows, you are to know that things are not so mixed up in things; but rather seeds common to many things must in many ways be mixed up and latent in things.

"But it often comes to pass on high mountains," you say, "that contiguous tops of tall trees rub together, the strong south winds constraining them so to do, until the flower of flame has broken out and they have burst into a blaze." Quite true and yet fire is not innate in woods; but there are many seeds of heat, and when they by rubbing have streamed together, they produce conflagrations in the forests. But if the flame was stored up ready made in the forests, the fire could not be concealed for any length of time, but would destroy forests, burn up trees indiscriminately. Do you now see, as we said a little before, that it often makes a very great difference with what things and in what position the same first-beginnings are held in union and what motions they mutually impart and receive, and that the same may when a little changed in arrangement produce, say, fires and a fir? Just as the words too consist of elements only a little changed in arrangement, though we denote firs and fires with two quite distinct names. Once again, if you suppose that whatever you perceive among visible things cannot be produced without imagining bodies of matter possessed of a like nature, in this way, you will find, the first-beginnings of things are destroyed: it will come to this, that they will be shaken by loud fits of convulsive laughter and will bedew with salt tears face and cheeks.

Now mark and learn what remains to be known and hear it

more distinctly. Nor does my mind fail to perceive how dark the things are; but the great hope of praise has smitten my heart with sharp thyrsus, and at the same time has struck into my breast sweet love of the muses, with which, now inspired, I traverse in blooming thought the pathless haunts of the Pierides never yet trodden by sole of man. I love to approach the untasted springs and to quaff, I love to cull fresh flowers and gather for my head a distinguished crown from spots whence the muses have yet veiled the brows of none; first because I teach of great things and essay to release the mind from the fast bonds of religious scruples, and next because on a dark subject I pen such lucid verses, o'erlaying all with the muses' charm. For that too would seem to be not without good grounds; but even as physicians, when they purpose to give nauseous wormwood to children, first smear the rim round the bowl with the sweet yellow juice of honey, that the unthinking age of children may be fooled as far as the lips, and meanwhile drink up the bitter draught of wormwood and though beguiled yet not be betrayed, but rather by such means recover health and strength; so I now, since this doctrine seems generally somewhat bitter to those by whom it has not been handled, and the multitude shrinks back from it in dismay, I have resolved to set forth to you our doctrine in sweet-toned Pierian verse and o'erlay it, as it were, with the pleasant honey of the muses, if haply by such means I might engage your mind on my verses, till such time as you clearly perceive with what shape the whole nature of things has been put together.

But since I have taught that most solid bodies of matter fly about forever unvanquished through all time, mark now, let us unfold whether there is or is not any limit to their sum; likewise let us clearly see whether that which has been found to be void, or room and space, in which things severally go on, is all of it altogether finite or stretches without limits and to an unfathomable depth.

Well then, the existing universe is bounded in none of its dimensions; for then it must have had an outside. Again, it is seen that there can be an outside of nothing, unless there be something beyond to bound it, so that that is seen, farther than which this our nature of sense does not follow the thing. Now since we must admit that there is nothing outside the sum, it has no outside, and therefore is without end and limit. And it matters not in which of its regions you take your stand; so invariably, whatever position anyone has taken up, he leaves the universe just as infinite as before in all directions. Again, if for the moment all existing space be held to be bounded, supposing a man runs forward to its outside borders and stands on the utmost verge and then throws a winged javelin; do you choose that it when hurled with vigorous force shall advance to the point to which it has been sent and fly to a distance, or do you decide that something can get in its way and stop it? For you must admit and adopt one of the two suppositions; either of which shuts you out from all escape and compels you to grant that the universe stretches without end. For whether there is something to get in its way and prevent its coming whither it was sent and placing itself in the point intended, or whether it is carried forward, in either case it has not started from the end. In this way I will go on and, wherever you have placed the outside borders, I will ask what then becomes of the javelin. The result will be that an end can nowhere be fixed, and that the room given for flight will still prolong the power of flight. Lastly, one thing is seen by the eyes to end another thing; air bounds off hills, and mountains air, earth limits sea and sea again all lands; the universe, however, there is nothing outside to end.

Again, if all the space of the whole sum were enclosed within fixed borders and were bounded, in that case the store of matter by its solid weights would have streamed together from all sides to the lowest point, nor could anything have gone on under the canopy of heaven, no, nor would there have been a heaven nor sunlight at all, inasmuch as all matter, settling down through infinite time past, would lie together in a heap. But as it is, sure enough no rest is given to the bodies of the first-beginnings, because there is no lowest point at all, to which they might stream together, as it were, and where they might take up their positions. All things are ever going on in ceaseless motion from all quarters and bodies of matter stirred to action are supplied from beneath out of infinite space. Therefore the nature of room and the space of the unfathomable void is such as bright thunderbolts cannot race through in their course though gliding on through endless tract of time, no, nor lessen one jot the journey that remains to go by all their travel: so huge a room is spread out on all sides for things without any bounds in all directions round.

Again, nature keeps the sum of things from setting any limit to itself, since she compels body to be ended by void and void in turn by body, so that either she thus renders the universe infinite by this alternation of the two, or else the one of the two, in case the other does not bound it, with its single nature stretches nevertheless immeasurably. [But void I have already proved to be infinite; therefore matter must be infinite: for if void were infinite and matter finite] neither sea nor earth nor the glittering quarters of heaven nor mortal kind nor the holy bodies of the gods could hold their ground one brief passing hour; since forced asunder from its union, the store of matter would be dissolved and borne along the mighty void, or rather I should say would never have combined to produce anything, since scattered abroad it could never have been brought together. For verily, not by design did the first-beginnings of things station themselves each in its right place guided by keen-sighted intelligence, nor did they bargain, sooth to say, what motions each should assume, but because many in number and shifting about in many ways throughout the universe they are driven and tormented by blows during infinite time past, after trying motions and unions of every kind at length they fall into arrangements such as those out of which this our sum of things has been formed, and by which too it is preserved through many great years when once it has been thrown into the appropriate motions, and causes the streams to replenish the greedy sea with copious river waters and the earth, fostered by the heat of the sun, to renew its produce, and the race of living things to come up and flourish, and the gliding fires of ether to live: all which these several things could in no wise bring to pass, unless a store of matter could rise up from infinite space, out of which store they are wont to make up in due season whatever has been lost. For as the nature of living things when robbed of food loses its body and wastes away, thus all things must be broken up, as soon as matter has ceased to be supplied, diverted in any way from its proper course. Nor can blows from without hold together all the sum which has been brought into union. They can, it is true, frequently strike upon and stay a part, until others come and the sum can be completed. At times, however, they are compelled to rebound and in so doing grant to the first-beginnings of things room and time for flight, to enable them to get clear away from the mass in union. Wherefore again and again, I repeat, many bodies must rise up; nay more, that the

blows themselves may not fail, there is need of an infinite supply of matter on all sides.

And herein, Memmius, be far from believing this, that all
things, as they say, press to the centre of the sum, and that for
this reason the nature of the world stands fast without any
strokes from the outside and the uppermost and lowest parts
cannot part asunder in any direction, because all things have
been always pressing towards the centre (if you can believe
that anything can rest upon itself); or that the heavy bodies
which are beneath the earth all press upwards and are at rest
on the earth, turned topsy-turvy, just like the images of things
which we see before us in the waters. In the same way too
they maintain that living things walk head downwards and
cannot tumble out of earth into the parts of heaven lying
below them any more than our bodies can spontaneously fly
into the quarters of heaven; that when those see the sun, we
behold the stars of night; and that they share with us time
about the seasons of heaven and pass nights equal in length to
our days. But groundless [error has devised such dreams] for
fools, because they have embraced [false principles of reason].
For there can be no centre [where the universe is] infinite; no
nor, even if there were a centre, could anything take up a
position there [any more on that account] than for some quite
different reason [be driven away]. For all room and space,
which we term void, must through centre, through no-centre
alike give place to heavy bodies, in whatever directions their
motions tend. Nor is there any spot of such a sort that when
bodies have reached it, they can lose their force of gravity and
stand upon void; and that, again, which is void must not serve
to support anything, but must, as its nature craves, continually
give place. Things cannot therefore in such a way be held in
union, o'ermastered by love of a centre.

Again, since they do not suppose that all bodies press to the
centre, but only those of earth and water, and such things as
are held together by a body of an earthly nature, the fluid of
the sea and great waters from the mountains; while on the
other hand, they teach that the subtle element of air and hot
fires at the same time are carried away from the centre and
that for this reason the whole ether round bickers with signs
and the sun's flame is fed throughout the blue of heaven, because heat flying from the centre all gathers together there,
and that the topmost boughs of trees could not put forth leaves

at all, unless from time to time [nature supplied] food from the earth to each, [their reasons are not only false, but they contradict each other. Space I have already proved to be infinite; and space, being infinite matter, as I have said, must also be infinite,] lest after the winged fashion of flames the walls of the world should suddenly break up and fly abroad along the mighty void, and all other things follow for like reasons and the innermost quarters of heaven tumble in from above and the earth in an instant withdraw from beneath our feet and amid the commingled ruins of things in it and of heaven, ruins unloosing the first bodies, should wholly pass away along the unfathomable void, so that in a moment of time not a wrack should be left behind, nothing save untenanted space and viewless first-beginnings. For on whatever side you shall first determine first bodies to be wanting, this side will be the gate of death for things, through this the whole crowd of matter will fling itself abroad.

If you will well learn these things, then carried to the end with slight trouble [you will be able by yourself to understand all the rest]. For one thing after another will grow clear and dark night will not rob you of the road, to keep you from surveying the utmost ends of nature: in such wise things will light the torch for other things.

UNITED BAPTIST BIBLE TRAINING SCHOOL
MONCTON, N. B.

Book Two

IT IS sweet, when on the great sea the winds trouble its waters, to behold from land another's deep distress; not that it is a pleasure and delight that any should be afflicted, but because it is sweet to see from what evils you are yourself exempt. It is sweet also to look upon the mighty struggles of war arrayed along the plains without sharing yourself in the danger. But nothing is more welcome than to hold the lofty and serene positions well fortified by the learning of the wise, from which you may look down upon others and see them wandering all abroad and going astray in their search for the path of life, see the contest among them of intellect, the rivalry of birth, the striving night and day with surpassing effort to struggle up to the summit of power and be masters of the world. O miserable minds of men! O blinded breasts! In what darkness of life and in how great dangers is passed all this term of life whatever its duration! Not choose to see that nature craves for itself nothing more than that the man from whose body pain holds aloof should in mind enjoy a feeling of pleasure exempt from care and fear? Therefore we see that for the body's nature but little is at all needed in order that such things as take away pain should be able to spread before us many delights as well. At times nature on her part wants no greater solace, although there are no golden images of youths through the house holding in their right hands flaming lamps, for supply of light to the nightly banquet, though the house shines not with silver nor glitters with gold nor do the panelled and gilded rooms re-echo to the harp—what time, though these things be wanting, they spread themselves in groups on the soft grass beside a stream of water under the boughs of a high tree and at no great cost pleasantly refresh their bodies, above all when the weather smiles and the

31

seasons of the year besprinkle the green grass with flowers. Nor do hot fevers sooner quit the body, if you toss about on pictured tapestry and blushing purple, than if you must lie under a poor man's blanket. Wherefore since treasures avail nothing in respect of our body nor birth nor the glory of kingly power, advancing farther you must hold that they are of no service to the mind as well; unless maybe when you see your legions swarm over the ground of the campus waging the mimicry of war, strengthened flank and rear by powerful reserves and great force of cavalry, and you marshall them equipped in arms and animated with one spirit, thereupon you find that religious scruples scared by these things fly panic-stricken from the mind; and that then fears of death leave the breast unembarrassed and free from care, when you see your fleet swarm forth and spread itself far and wide. But if we see that these things are food for laughter and mere mockeries, and in good truth the fears of men and dogging cares dread not the clash of arms and cruel weapons, if unabashed they mix among kings and caesars and stand not in awe of the glitter from gold nor the brilliant sheen of the purple robe, how can you doubt that this is wholly the prerogative of reason, when the whole of life withal is a struggle in the dark? For even as children are flurried and dread all things in the thick darkness, thus we in the daylight fear at times things not a whit more to be dreaded than those which children shudder at in the dark and fancy sure to be. This terror, therefore, and darkness of mind must be dispelled not by the rays of the sun and glittering shafts of day, but by the aspect and law of nature.

Now mark and I will explain by what motion the begetting bodies of matter do beget different things and after they are begotten again break them up, and by what force they are compelled so to do and what velocity is given to them for travelling through the great void: do you mind to give heed to my words. For verily matter does not cohere inseparably massed together, since we see that everything wanes and perceive that all things ebb, as it were, by length of time and that age withdraws them from our sight, though yet the sum is seen to remain unimpaired by reason that the bodies which quit each thing lessen the things from which they go, gift with increase those to which they have come, compel the former to grow old, the latter to come to their prime, and yet abide not with these. Thus the sum of things is ever renewed and mortals live by a reciprocal dependency. Some nations wax, others wane, and in a brief space the races of living things are changed and, like runners, hand over the lamp of life.

If you think that first-beginnings of things can stop and by stopping give birth to new motions of things, you wander far astray from the path of true reason: since they travel about through void, the first-beginnings of things must all move on either by their own weight or haply by the stroke of another. For when during motion they have, as often happens, met and clashed, the result is a sudden rebounding in an opposite direction; and no wonder, since they are most hard and of weight proportioned to their solidity, and nothing behind gets in their way. And that you may more clearly see that all bodies of matter are in restless movement, remember that there is no lowest point in the sum of the universe, and that first bodies have not where to take their stand, since space is without end and limit and extends immeasurably in all directions round, as I have shown in many words and as has been proved by sure reason. Since this then is a certain truth, sure enough, no rest is given to first bodies throughout the unfathomable void, but driven on rather in ceaseless and varied motion, they partly, after they have pressed together, rebound, leaving great spaces between, while in part they are so dashed away after the stroke as to leave but small spaces between. And all that form a denser aggregation when brought together and rebound leaving trifling spaces between, held fast by their own close-tangled shapes, these form enduring bases of stone and unyielding bodies of iron and suchlike. But those which spring far off and rebound far, leaving great spaces between, these furnish us with thin air and bright sunlight. And many more travel along the great void, which have been thrown off from the unions of things, or, though admitted, have yet in no case been able likewise to assimilate their motions. Of this truth, even as I relate it, we have a representation and picture always going on before our eyes and present to us: observe whenever the rays are let in and pour the sunlight through the dark chambers of houses: you will see many minute bodies in many ways through the apparent void mingle in the midst of the light of the rays, and as in never-ending conflict skirmish and give battle, combatting in troops and never halting, driven about in frequent meetings and partings; so that you may guess from this what it is for first-beginnings of things to be ever tossing about in the great void. So far as it goes, a small thing may give an illustration of great things and put you on the track of knowledge. And for this reason too it is meet that you should give greater heed to these bodies which are seen to tumble about in the sun's rays, because such tumblings imply that motions also of matter latent and unseen are at the bottom. For you will observe many things there impelled by unseen blows to change their course and, driven back, to return the way they came, now this way, now that way in all directions round. All, you are to know, derive this restlessness from the first-beginnings. For the first-beginnings of things move first of themselves; next those bodies which form a small aggregate and come nearest, so to say, to the powers of the first-beginnings are impelled and set in movement by the unseen strokes of those first bodies, and they in turn stir up bodies which are a little larger. Thus motion mounts up from the first-beginnings and step by step issues forth to our senses, so that those bodies also move which we can discern in the sunlight, though it is not clearly seen by what blows they so act.

Now what velocity is given to bodies of matter, you may apprehend, Memmius, in few words from this: when morning first sprinkles the earth with fresh light and the different birds flitting about the pathless woods through the buxom air fill all places with their clear notes, we see it to be plain and evident to all how suddenly the sun after rising is wont at such a time to overspread all things and clothe them with his light. But that heat which the sun emits and that bright light pass not through empty void; and therefore they are forced to travel more slowly, until they cleave through the waves, so to speak, of air. Nor do the several minute bodies of heat pass on one by one, but closely entangled and massed together; whereby at one and the same time they are pulled back by one another and are impeded from without, so that they are forced to travel more slowly. But the first-beginnings which are of solid singleness, when they pass through empty void and nothing delays them from without and they themselves, single from the nature of their parts, are borne with headlong endeavour towards the one single spot to which their efforts tend, must sure enough surpass in velocity and be carried along much more swiftly than the light of the sun, and race through many times the extent of space in the same time in which the beams of the sun fill the heaven throughout. . . . nor follow up the several first-beginnings to see by what law each thing goes on.

But some, in opposition to this, being ignorant of matter, believe that nature cannot without the providence of the gods in such nice conformity to the ways of men vary the seasons of the year and bring forth crops, ay and procure all the other things which divine pleasure, the guide of life, prompts men to approach, escorting them in person and enticing them by her fondlings to continue their races through the arts of Venus, that mankind may not come to an end. Now when they suppose that the gods designed all things for the sake of men, they seem to me in all respects to have strayed most widely from true reason. For even if I did not know what first-beginnings are, yet this, judging by the very arrangements of heaven, I would venture to affirm, and led by many other circumstances to maintain: that the nature of the world has by no means been made for us by divine power, so great are the defects with which it stands encumbered. All which, Memmius, we will hereafter make clear to you; we will now go on to explain what remains to be told of motions.

Now methinks is the place herein to prove this point also, that no bodily thing can by its own power be borne upwards and travel upwards; that the bodies of flames may not in this matter lead you into error. For they are begotten with an upward tendency, and in the same direction receive increase, and goodly crops and trees grow upwards, though their weights, so far as in them is, all tend downwards. And when fires leap to the roofs of houses and with swift flame lick up rafters and beams, we are not to suppose that they do so spontaneously without a force pushing them up. Even thus blood discharged from our body spirts out and springs up on high and scatters gore about. See you not too with what force the liquid of water spits out logs and beams? The more we have pushed and forced them deep down and have pressed them in, many of us together, with all our might and much painful effort, with the greater avidity it vomits them up and casts them forth, so that they rise and start out more than half their length. And yet methinks we doubt not that these, so far as in them is, are all borne downwards through the empty void. In the same way flames also ought to be able, when squeezed out, to mount upward through the air, although their weights, so far as in them is, strive to draw them down. See you not too that the nightly meteors of heaven as they fly aloft draw after them long trails of flames in whatever direction nature has given them a passage? Do you not perceive stars and meteors fall to the earth? The sun also from the height of heaven sheds its heat on all sides and sows the fields with light; to the earth therefore as well the sun's heat tends. Lightnings also you see fly athwart the rains: now from this side, now from that, fires burst from the clouds and rush about; the force of flame falls to the earth all round.

This point too herein we wish you to apprehend: when bodies are borne downwards sheer through void, at quite uncertain times and uncertain points of space they swerve a little from their equal poise: you just and only just can call it a change of inclination. If they were not used to swerve, they all would fall down, like drops of rain, through the deep void, and no clashing would have been begotten nor blow produced among the first-beginnings: thus nature never would have produced aught.

But if haply anyone believes that heavier bodies, as they are carried more quickly sheer through space, can fall from above on the lighter and so beget blows able to produce begetting motions, he goes most widely astray from true reason. For whenever bodies fall through water and thin air, they must quicken their descents in proportion to their weights, because the body of water and subtle nature of air cannot retard everything in equal degree, but more readily give way, overpowered by the heavier; on the other hand, empty void cannot offer resistance to anything in any direction at any time, but must, as its nature craves, continually give way; and for this reason all things must be moved and borne along with equal velocity, though of unequal weights, through the unresisting void. Therefore heavier things will never be able to fall from above on lighter nor of themselves to beget blows sufficient to produce the varied motions by which nature carries on things. Wherefore again and again I say bodies must swerve a little; and yet not more than the least possible; lest we be found to be imagining oblique motions and this the reality should refute. For this we see to be plain and evident, that weights, so far as in them is, cannot travel obliquely, when they fall from above, at least so far as you can perceive; but that nothing swerves in any case from the straight course, who is there that can perceive?

Again, if all motion is ever linked together and a new motion ever springs from another in a fixed order and first-beginnings do not by swerving make some commencement of motion to break through the decrees of fate, that cause follow not cause from everlasting, whence have all living creatures here on earth, whence, I ask, has been wrested from the fates the power by which we go forward whither the will leads each, by which likewise we change the direction of our motions neither at a fixed time nor fixed place, but when and where the mind itself has prompted? For beyond a doubt in these things his own will makes for each a beginning and from this beginning motions are welled through the limbs. See you not too, when the barriers are thrown open at a given moment, that yet the eager powers of the horses cannot start forward so instantaneously as the mind itself desires? The whole store of matter through the whole body must be sought out, in order that, stirred up through all the frame, it may follow with undivided effort the bent of the mind; so that you see the beginning of motion is born from the heart, and the action first commences in the will of the mind and next is transmitted through the whole body and frame. Quite different is the case when we move on propelled by a stroke inflicted by the strong might and strong compulsion of another; for then it is quite clear that all the matter of the whole body moves and is hurried on against our inclination, until the will has reined it in throughout the limbs. Do you see then in this case that, though an outward force often pushes men on and compels them frequently to advance against their will and to be hurried headlong on, there yet is something in our breast sufficient to struggle against and resist it? And when too this something chooses, the store of matter is compelled sometimes to change its course through the limbs and frame, and after it has been forced forward, is reined in and settles back into its place. Wherefore in seeds too you must admit the same, admit that besides blows and weights there is another cause of motions, from which this power of free action has been begotten in us, since we see that nothing can come from nothing. For weight forbids that all things be done by blows through, as it were, an outward force; but that the mind itself does not feel an internal necessity in all its actions and is not, as it were, overmastered and compelled to bear and put up with this, is caused by a minute swerving of first-beginnings at no fixed part of space and no fixed time.

Nor was the store of matter ever more closely massed nor held apart by larger spaces between; for nothing is either added to its bulk or lost to it. Wherefore the bodies of the first-beginnings in time gone by moved in the same way in which now they move, and will ever hereafter be borne along in like manner, and the things which have been wont to be begotten will be begotten after the same law and will be and will grow and will wax in strength so far as is given to each by the decrees of nature. And no force can change the sum of things; for there is nothing outside, either into which any kind of matter can escape out of the universe or out of which a new supply can arise and burst into the universe and change all the nature of things and alter their motions.

And herein you need not wonder at this, that though the first-beginnings of things are all in motion, yet the sum is seen to rest in supreme repose, unless where a thing exhibits motions with its individual body. For all the nature of first things lies far away from our senses beneath their ken; and therefore since they are themselves beyond what you can see, they must withdraw from sight their motions as well; and the more so that the things which we can see do yet often conceal their motions when a great distance off. Thus often the woolly flocks, as they crop the glad pastures on a hill, creep on whither the grass jewelled with fresh dew summons and invites each, and the lambs, fed to the full, gambol and playfully butt; all which objects appear to us from a distance to be blended together and to rest like a white spot on a green hill. Again, when mighty legions fill with their movements all parts of the plains, waging the mimicry of war, the glitter then lifts itself up to the sky and the whole earth round gleams with brass, and beneath a noise is raised by the mighty trampling of men and the mountains, stricken by the shouting, re-echo the voices to the stars of heaven, and horsemen fly about and, suddenly wheeling, scour across the middle of the plains, shaking them with the vehemence of their charge. And yet there is some spot on the high hills, seen from which they appear to stand still and to rest on the plains as a bright spot.

Now mark and next in order apprehend of what kind and

how widely differing in their forms are the beginnings of all things, how varied by manifold diversities of shape; not that a scanty number are possessed of a like form, but because as a rule they do not all resemble one the other. And no wonder; for since there is so great a store of them that, as I have shown, there is no end or sum, they must sure enough not one and all be marked by an equal bulk and like shape, one with another. The race of man vouches the fact and the mute swimming shoals of the scaly tribes and the blithe herds and wild beasts and the different birds which haunt the gladdening watering spots about riverbanks and springs and pools, and those which flit about and throng the pathless woods: go and take any one you like in any one kind, and you will yet find that they differ in their shapes, every one from every other. And in no other way could child recognise mother or mother child; and this we see that they all can do, and that they are just as well known to one another as human beings are. Thus often in front of the beauteous shrines of the gods a calf falls sacrificed beside the incense-burning altars, and spirts from its breast a warm stream of blood; but the bereaved mother as she ranges over the green lawns knows the footprints stamped on the ground by the cloven hoofs, scanning with her eyes every spot to see if she can anywhere behold her lost youngling: then she fills with her moanings the leafy wood as she desists from her search and again and again goes back to the stall, pierced to the heart by the loss of her calf; nor can the soft willows and grass quickened with dew and those rivers gliding level with their banks comfort her mind and put away the care that has entered into her, nor can other forms of calves throughout the glad pastures divert her mind and ease it of its care: so persistently she seeks something special and known. Again, the tender kids with their shaking voices know their horned dams and the butting lambs the flocks of bleating sheep: thus they run, as nature craves, each without fail to its own udder of milk. Lastly, in the case of any kind of corn you like, you will yet find that any one grain is not so similar to any other in the same kind, but that there runs through them some difference to distinguish the forms. On a like principle of difference we see the class of shells paint the lap of earth, where the sea with gentle waves beats on the thirsty sand of the winding shore. Therefore again and again I say it is necessary for like reasons that first-beginnings of things, since they exist by nature and are not made by hand after the exact model of one, should fly about with shapes in some cases differing one from the other.

It is right easy for us on such a principle to explain why the fire of lightning has much more power to pierce than ours which is born of earthly pinewood: you may say that the heavenly fire of lightning, subtle as it is, is formed of smaller shapes and therefore passes through openings which this our fire cannot pass, born as it is of woods and sprung from pine. Again, light passes through horn, but rain is thrown off. Why, if not that those first bodies of light are smaller than those of which the nurturing liquid of water is made. And quickly as we see wines flow through a strainer, sluggish oil, on the other hand, is slow to do so, because, sure enough, it consists of elements either larger in size or more hooked and tangled in one another, and therefore it is that the first-beginnings of things cannot so readily be separated from each other and severally stream through the several openings of any thing.

Moreover, the liquids honey and milk excite a pleasant sensation of tongue when held in the mouth; but on the other hand, the nauseous nature of wormwood and of harsh centaury writhes the mouth with a noisome flavour; so that you may easily see that the things which are able to affect the senses pleasantly consist of smooth and round elements; while all those, on the other hand, which are found to be bitter and harsh are held in connexion by particles that are more hooked and for this reason are wont to tear open passages into our senses and in entering in to break through the body.

All things, in short, which are agreeable to the senses and all which are unpleasant to the feeling are mutually repugnant, formed as they are out of an unlike first shape; lest haply you suppose that the harsh grating of the creaking saw consists of elements as smooth as those of tuneful melodies which musicians wake into life with nimble fingers and give shape to on strings; or suppose that the first-beginnings are of like shape which pass into the nostrils of men, when noisome carcases are burning, and when the stage is fresh sprinkled with Cilician saffron, while the altar close by exhales Panchaean odours; or decide that the pleasant colours of things which are able to feast the eyes are formed of a seed like to the seed of those which make the pupil smart and force it to shed tears or from their disgusting aspect look

hideous and foul. For every shape which gratifies the senses
has been formed not without a smoothness in its elements;
but on the other hand, whatever is painful and harsh has
been produced not without some roughness of matter. There
are too some elements which are with justice thought to be
neither smooth nor altogether hooked with barbed points, but
rather to have minute angles slightly projecting, such as can
tickle rather than hurt the senses; of which class tartar of wine
is formed and the flavours of elecampane. Again, that hot
fires and cold frost have fangs of a dissimilar kind wherewith
to pierce the senses is proved to us by the touch of each. For
touch, touch, ye holy divinities of the gods, is feeling of the
body, either when an extraneous thing makes its way in, or
when a thing which is born in the body hurts it, or gives
pleasure as it issues forth by the birth-bestowing ways of
Venus, or when from some collision the seeds are disordered
within the body and distract the feeling by their mutual
disturbance; as if haply you were yourself to strike with the
hand any part of the body you please and so make trial.
Wherefore the shapes of the first-beginnings must differ
widely, since they are able to give birth to different feelings.

Again, things which look to us hard and dense must consist
of particles more hooked together, and be held in union because welded all through with branch-like elements. In this
class first of all diamond stones stand in foremost line inured
to despise blows, and stout blocks of basalt and the strength
of hard iron and brass bolts which scream out as they hold
fast to their staples. Those things which are liquid and of
fluid body ought to consist more of smooth and round elements; for the several drops have no mutual cohesion and
their onward course too has a ready flow downwards. All
things, lastly, which you see disperse themselves in an instant,
as smoke mists and flames, if they do not consist entirely of
smooth and round, must yet not be held fast by closely
tangled elements, so that they may be able to pierce the body
and enter into loose substances, yet not stick together: thus
you may easily know that whatever we see in this way conveyed to the senses consists not of tangled but of pointed
elements. Do not, however, hold it to be wonderful that some
things which are fluid you see to be likewise bitter, for instance the sea's moisture: because it is fluid, it consists of
smooth and round particles, and many rough bodies mixed

up with these produce pains; and yet they must not be
hooked so as to hold together: you are to know that though
rough, they are yet spherical, so that while they roll freely
on, they may at the same time hurt the senses. And that you
may more readily believe that with smooth are mixed rough
first-beginnings from which Neptune's body is made bitter,
there is a way of separating these, and of seeing how the fresh
water, when it is often filtered through the earth, flows by
itself into a trench and sweetens; for it leaves above the first-
beginnings of the nauseous saltness, inasmuch as the rough
particles can more readily stay behind in the earth.

And now that I have shown this, I will go on to link to it
a truth which depends on this and from this draws its proof:
the first-beginnings of things have different shapes, but the
number of shapes is finite. If this were not so, then once
more it would follow that some seeds must be of infinite bulk
of body. For since in one and the same small size of any first
body you like the shapes cannot vary much from one another
—say, for instance, the first bodies consist of three least parts,
or augment them by a few more; when, to wit, in all possible
ways, by placing each in turn at the top and at the bottom, by
making the right change places with the left, you shall have
tried all those parts of one first body and found what manner
of shape each different arrangement gives to the whole of that
body, if after all this haply you shall wish still to vary the
shapes, you will have to add other parts: it will next follow
that for like reasons the arrangement will require other parts,
if haply you shall wish still again to vary the shapes—from
all this it results that increase of bulk in the body follows upon
newness of the shapes. Wherefore you cannot possibly believe
that seeds have an infinite variety of forms, lest you force some
to be of a monstrous hugeness, which as I have above shown
cannot be proved. Moreover, I tell you, barbaric robes and radiant Meliboean purple dipped in Thessalian dye of shells [and
the hues which are displayed] by the golden brood of pea-
cocks steeped in laughing beauty would all be thrown aside,
surpassed by some new colour of things; the smell of myrrh
would be despised and the flavours of honey, and the melodies
of the swan and Phoebean tunes set off by the varied play of
strings would in like sort be suppressed and silenced; for
something ever would arise more surpassing than the rest. All
things likewise might fall back into worse states, even as we

have said they might advance to better; for reversely too, one thing would be more noisome than all other things to nostril, ear and eye and taste. Now since these things are not so, but a fixed limit has been assigned to things which bounds their sum on each side, you must admit that matter also has a finite number of different shapes. Once more from summer fires to chill frosts a definite path is traced out and in like manner is again travelled back; for cold and heat lie on the outside, and moderate warmths midway between both, filling up in succession the sum. Therefore things produced differ by finite degrees, since on each side they are marked off by points, one at one, another at the other end, molested on the one hand by flames, on the other by stiffening frosts.

And now that I have shown this, I will go on to link to it a truth which depends on this and from this draws its proof: the first-beginnings of things which have a like shape one with the other are infinite in number. For since the difference of forms is finite, those which are like must be infinite or the sum of matter will be finite, which I proved not to be the case, when I showed in my verses that the minute bodies of matter from everlasting continually uphold the sum of things through an uninterrupted succession of blows on all sides. For though you see that some animals are rarer than others and discern a less fruitful nature in them, yet in another quarter and spot and in distant lands there may be many of that kind and the full tale may be made up; just as we see that in the class of four-footed beasts snake-handed elephants are elsewhere especially numerous; for India is so fenced about with an ivory rampart made out of many thousands of these, that its inner parts cannot be reached, so great is the quantity of brutes, of which we see but very few samples. But yet though I should grant this point too—be there even as you will some one thing sole in its kind existing alone with a body that had birth, and let no other thing resemble it in the whole world—yet unless there shall be an infinite supply of matter out of which it may be conceived and brought into being, it cannot be produced, and, more than this, it cannot have growth and food. For though I should assume this point also, that birth-giving bodies of some one thing are tossed about in finite quantity throughout the universe, whence, where, by what force and in what way shall they meet together and combine in so vast a sea, such an alien medley of matter?

They have, methinks, no way of uniting; but even as when great and numerous shipwrecks have occurred, the great sea is wont to tumble about banks, rudders, yards, prow masts and swimming oars, so that poopfittings are seen floating about along every shore and utter to mortals a warning to try to shun the snares and violence and guile of the faithless sea, and never at any time to trust to it, when the winning face of calm ocean laughs treacherously; thus too if you shall once decide that certain first-beginnings are finite, different currents of matter must scatter and tumble them about through all time, so that they can never be brought into union and combine, nor abide in any union nor grow up and increase. But plain matter of fact shows that each of these results manifestly does take place, that things can be brought into being and when begotten advance in growth. It is clear then that in any class you like the first-beginnings of things are infinite, out of which all supplies are furnished.

Thus, then, neither can death-dealing motions keep the mastery always nor entomb existence forevermore, nor, on the other hand, can the birth- and increase-giving motions of things preserve them always after they are born. Thus the war of first-beginnings waged from eternity is carried on with dubious issue; now here, now there, the life-bringing elements of things get the mastery and are o'ermastered in turn: with the funeral wail is blended the cry which babies raise when they enter the borders of light; and no night ever followed day nor morning night that heard not mingling with the sickly infant's cries wailings, the attendants on death and black funeral.

And herein it is proper you should keep under seal, and guard, there consigned, in faithful memory this truth, that there is nothing whose nature is apparent to sense, which consists of one kind of first-beginnings; nothing which is not formed by a mixing of seed. And whenever a thing possesses in itself in larger measure many powers and properties, in that measure it shows that there are in it the greatest number of different kinds and varied shapes of first-beginnings. First of all, the earth has in her first bodies out of which springs, rolling coolness along, replenish without fail the boundless sea; she has bodies out of which fires rise up; for in many spots the earth's crust is on fire and burns, though headstrong Etna rages with fires of surpassing force. Then too she has bodies out of which she can raise for mankind goodly crops and joyous trees, out of which too she can supply to the mountain-ranging race of wild beasts rivers, leaves and glad pastures. Wherefore she has alone been named great mother of gods and mother of beasts and parent of our body.

Of her the old and learned poets of the Greeks have sung, that [borne aloft on high-raised] seat in a chariot, she drives a pair of lions, teaching that the great earth hangs in the expanse of air and that earth cannot rest on earth. To her chariot they have yoked wild beasts, because a brood however savage ought to be tamed and softened by the kind offices of parents. They have encircled the top of her head with a mural crown, because fortified in choice positions she sustains towns; adorned with which emblem the image of the divine mother is carried nowadays through wide lands in awe-inspiring state. Different nations after old-established ritual term her Idean mother, and give her for escort Phrygian bands, because they tell that from those lands corn first began to be produced throughout the world. They assign her galli, because they would show by this type that they who had done violence to the divinity of the mother and have proved ungrateful to their parents are to be deemed unworthy to bring a living offspring into the borders of light. Tight-stretched tambourines and hollow cymbals resound all round to the stroke of their open hands, and horns menace with hoarse-sounding music, and the hollow pipe stirs their minds in Phrygian mood. They carry weapons before them, emblems of furious rage, meet to fill the thankless souls and godless breasts of the rabble with terror for the divinity of the goddess. Therefore when, first borne in procession through great cities, she mutely enriches mortals with a blessing not expressed in words, they strew all her path with brass and silver, presenting her with bounteous alms, and scatter over her a snow-shower of roses, o'ershadowing the mother and her troops of attendants. Here an armed band to whom the Greeks give the name of Phrygian Curetes, in that it haply joins in the game of arms and springs up in measure all dripping with blood, shaking with its nodding the frightful crests upon the head, represents the Dictaean Curetes who, as the story is, erst drowned in Crete that infant cry of Jove, when the young band about the young babe in rapid dance, arms in hand, to measured tread beat brass on brass, that

Saturn might not get him to consign to his devouring jaws and stab the mother to the heart with a never-healing wound. For these reasons they escort in arms the great mother, or else because they mean by this sign that the goddess preaches to men to be willing with arms and valour to defend their country and be ready to be a safeguard and an ornament to their parents. All which, well and beautifully as it is set forth and told, is yet widely removed from true reason. For the nature of gods must ever in itself of necessity enjoy immortality together with supreme repose, far removed and withdrawn from our concerns; since exempt from every pain, exempt from all dangers, strong in its own resources, not wanting aught of us, it is neither gained by favours nor moved by anger. And here if anyone thinks proper to call the sea Neptune and corn Ceres and chooses rather to misuse the name of Bacchus than to utter the term that belongs to that liquor, let us allow him to declare that the earth is mother of the gods, if he only forbear in earnest to stain his mind with foul religion. The earth, however, is at all time without feeling, and because it receives into it the first-beginnings of many things, it brings them forth in many ways into the light of the sun.

And so the wooly flocks and the martial breed of horses and horned herds, though often cropping the grass from one field beneath the same canopy of heaven and slaking their thirst from one stream of water, yet have all their life a dissimilar appearance and retain the nature of their parents and severally imitate their ways each after its kind: so great is the diversity of matter in any kind of herbage, so great in every river. And hence too anyone you please out of the whole number of living creatures is made up of bones, blood, veins, heat, moisture, flesh, sinews; and these things again differ widely from one another and are composed of first-beginnings of unlike shape. Furthermore, whatever things are set on fire and burned, store up in their body, if nothing else, at least those particles, out of which they may radiate fire and send out light and make sparks fly and scatter embers all about. If you will go over all other things by a like process of reasoning, you will thus find that they conceal in their body the seeds of many things and contain elements of various shapes. Again you see many things to which are given at once both colour and taste together with smell. These several properties in each thing must therefore be made up of elements of different shapes; for smell enters in where colour passes not into the frame, colour too in one way, taste in another makes its way into the senses; so that you know they differ in the particular shapes of their elements. Therefore unlike forms unite into one mass and things are made up of a mixture of seed. Throughout, moreover, these very verses of ours you see many elements common to many words, though yet you must admit that the verses and words one with another are different and composed of different elements; not that but few letters which are in common run through them or that no two words or verses one with another are made up entirely of the same, but because as a rule they do not all resemble one the other. Thus also, though in other things there are many first-beginnings common to many things, yet they can make up one with the other a quite dissimilar whole; so that men and corn and joyous trees may fairly be said to consist of different elements.

And yet we are not to suppose that all things can be joined together in all ways; for then you would see prodigies produced on all hands, forms springing up half man, half beast, and sometimes tall boughs sprouting from the living body, and many limbs of land creatures joined with those of sea animals, nature too throughout the all-bearing lands feeding chimeras which breathed flames from hideous mouth. It is plain, however, that nothing of the sort is done, since we see that all things produced from fixed seeds and a fixed mother can in growing preserve the marks of their kind. This, you are to know, must take place after a fixed law. For the particles suitable for each thing from all kinds of food when inside the body pass into the frame, and joining on, produce the appropriate motions; but on the other hand, we see nature throw out on the earth those that are alien, and many things with their unseen bodies fly out of the body impelled by blows: those I mean which have not been able to join onto any part nor when inside to feel in unison with and adopt the vital motions. But lest you haply suppose that living things alone are bound by these conditions, such a law keeps all things within their limits. For even as things begotten are in their whole nature all unlike one the other, thus each must consist of first-beginnings of unlike shape; not that a scanty number are possessed of a like form, but because as a rule they do not all resemble one the other. Again, since the seeds differ, there must be a difference in the spaces between, the passages, the connexions, the weights, the blows, the clashings, the motions; all which not only disjoin living bodies, but hold apart the lands and the whole sea, and keep the whole heaven away from the earth.

Now mark, and apprehend precepts amassed by my welcome toil, lest haply you deem that those things which you see with your eyes to be bright, because white are formed of white principles, or that the things which are black are born from black seed; or that things which are steeped in any other colour bear that colour because the bodies of matter are dyed with a colour like to it. For the bodies of matter have no colour at all either like to the things or unlike. But if haply it seems to you that no impression of the mind can throw itself into these bodies, you wander far astray. For since men born blind, who have never beheld the light of the sun, do yet know bodies by touch, you are to know that bodies can fall under the ken of our mind too, though stained with no colour. Again, whatever things we ourselves touch in the thick darkness, we do not perceive to be dyed with any colour. And since I prove that this is the case, I will now show that there are things linked to no colour from the beginning of time. Well, any colour without any exception changes into any other; and this first-beginnings ought in no wise to do: something unchangeable must remain over, that all things be not utterly reduced to nothing. For whenever a thing changes and quits its proper limits, at once this change of state is the death of that which was before. Therefore mind not to dye with colour the seeds of things, that you may not have all things altogether returning to nothing.

Moreover, if no quality of colour is assigned to first-beginnings and they are yet possessed of varied shapes out of which they beget colours of every kind and change them about by reason that it makes a great difference with what other seeds and in what position the seeds are severally held in union and what motions they mutually impart and receive, you can explain at once with the greatest ease why those things which just before were of a black colour may become all at once of marble whiteness; as the sea, when mighty winds have stirred up its waters, is changed into white waves of the brightness of marble: you may say that when the matter of that which we often see to be black has been mixed up anew and the arrangement of its first-beginnings has been changed and some have been added and some been taken away, the immediate result is that it appears bright and white. But if the waters of the sea consisted of azure seeds, they could in no wise become white; for however much you jumble together seeds which are azure, they can never pass into a marble colour. But if the seeds which make up the one unmixed brightness of the sea are dyed some with one, some with other colours, just as often out of different forms and varied shapes something square and of a uniform figure is made up, in that case it were natural that as we see unlike forms contained in the square, so we should see in the water of the sea or in any other one and unmixed brightness colours widely unlike and different to one another. Moreover the unlike figures do not in the least hinder or prevent the whole figure from being a square on the outside; but the various colours of things are a let and hindrance to the whole things being of a uniform brightness.

Then too the reason which leads and draws us on sometimes to assign colours to the first-beginnings of things falls to the ground, since white things are not produced from white, nor those which are black from black, but out of things of various colours. For white things will much more readily rise up and be born from no colour than from a black or any other colour which thwarts and opposes it.

Moreover, since colours cannot exist without light and first-beginnings of things do not come out into the light, you may be sure they are clothed with no colour. For what colour can there be in total darkness? Nay, it changes in the light itself according as its brightness comes from a straight or slanting stroke of light. After this fashion the down which encircles and crowns the nape and throat of doves shows itself in the sun: at one time it is ruddy with the hue of bright pyropus; at another it appears by a certain way of looking at it to blend with coral-red green emeralds. The tail of the peacock, when it is saturated with abundant light, changes in like fashion its colours as it faces the sun. And since these colours are begotten by a certain stroke of light, sure enough you must believe that they cannot be produced without it. And since the pupil receives into it a kind of blow when it is said to perceive a white colour, and then another when it perceives black or any other colour, and since it is of no moment with what colour the things which you touch are provided, but rather with what sort of shape they are furnished, you are to know that first-beginnings have no need of colours, but give forth sensations of touch varying according to their various shapes.

Moreover, since no particular kind of colour is assigned to particular shapes and every configuration of first-beginnings can exist in any colour, why on a like principle are not the things which are formed out of them in every kind o'erlaid with colours of every kind? For then it were natural that crows too in flying should often display a white colour from white wings and that swans should come to be black from a black seed, or of any other different colour you please.

Again, the more minute the parts are into which anything is rent, the more you may perceive the colour fade away by little and little and become extinct; as for instance if a piece of purple is torn into small shreds: when it has been plucked into separate threads, the purple and the scarlet, far the most brilliant of colours, are quite effaced; from which you may infer that the shreds part with all their colour before they come back to the seeds of things.

Lastly, since you admit that all bodies do not utter a voice nor emit a smell, for this reason you do not assign to all sounds and smells. So also since we cannot perceive all things with the eyes, you are to know that some things are as much denuded of colour as others are without smell and devoid of sound, and that the keen-discerning mind can just as well apprehend these things as it can take note of things which are destitute of other qualities.

But lest haply you suppose that first bodies remain stripped of colour alone, they are also wholly devoid of warmth and cold and violent heat, and are judged to be barren of sound and drained of moisture, and emit from their body no scent of their own. Just as when you set about preparing the balmy liquid of sweet marjoram and myrrh and the flower of spikenard, which gives forth to the nostrils a scent like nectar; before all you should seek, so far as you may and can find it, the substance of scentless oil, such as gives out no perfumes to the nostrils, that it may as little as possible meddle with and destroy by its own pungency the odours mixed in its body and boiled up with it; for the same reason the first-beginnings of things must not bring to the begetting of things a smell or sound of their own, since they cannot discharge anything from themselves, and for the same reason no taste either, nor cold nor any heat, moderate or violent, and the like. For as these things, be they what they may, are still liable to death, whether pliant with a soft, brittle with a crumbling, or hollow with a porous body, they must all be withdrawn from the first-beginnings, if we wish to assign to things imperishable foundations for the whole sum of existence to rest upon: that you may not have things returning altogether to nothing.

To come to another point, whatever things we perceive to have sense, you must yet admit to be all composed of senseless first-beginnings: manifest tokens which are open to all to apprehend, so far from refuting or contradicting this, do rather themselves take us by the hand and constrain us to believe that, as I say, living things are begotten from senseless things. We may see, in fact, living worms spring out of stinking dung, when the soaked earth has gotten putridity after excessive rains; and all things besides change in the same way: rivers, leaves and glad pastures change into cattle, cattle change their substance into our bodies, and often out of these the powers of wild beasts and the bodies of the strong of wing are increased. Therefore nature changes all foods into living bodies and engenders out of them all the senses of living creatures, much in the same way as she dissolves dry woods into flames and converts all things into fires. Now do you see that it is of great moment in what sort of arrangement the first-beginnings of things are severally placed and with what others they are mixed up, when they impart and receive motions?

Then again, what is that which strikes your mind, which affects that mind and constrains it to give utterance to many different thoughts, to save you from believing that the sensible is begotten out of senseless things? Sure enough, it is because stones and wood and earth, however mixed together, are yet unable to produce vital sense. This therefore it will be well to remember herein, that I do not assert that the sensible and sensations are forthwith begotten out of all things without exception which produce things; but that it is of great moment first how minute the particles are which make up the sensible thing and then what shape they possess and what, in short, they are in their motions, arrangements, positions. None of which requisites we find in woods and clods; and yet even these things, when they have, so to speak, become rotten through the rains, bring forth worms, because bodies of matter driven from their ancient arrangements by a new condition are combined in the same way as when living creatures are to be begotten. Next, they who hold that the sensible can be produced anew out of other sensible things, in that case suppose those things, accustomed thus to have sense, to be soft; for all sense is bound up with flesh, sinews, veins; which in everything we see to be soft and formed of a mortal body. But even suppose that these things can remain eternal: they must yet, I presume, either have the sense of some part or else be deemed to possess a sense similar to the entire living creatures. But the parts cannot possibly have sense by themselves alone; for all sense of the different members has reference to something else; nor can the hand when severed from us nor any other part of the body whatever by itself maintain sensation. It remains to assume that they resemble the entire living creatures. In this case it is necessary that they should feel the things which we feel in the same way as we do, in order that they may be able in all points to work in concert with the vital sense. How then can they be called first-beginnings of things and shun the paths of death, seeing that they are living things, and that living things are one and the same with mortal things? Nay, granting they could do this, yet by their meeting and union they will make nothing but a jumble and medley of living things; just, you are to know, as men, cattle and wild beasts would be unable to beget any other thing by all their mixing with one another. But if haply they lose from their body their own sense and adopt another, what use was it to assign what is again withdrawn? Moreover, the instance to which we had before recourse, inasmuch as we see the eggs of fowls change into living chicks and worms burst forth, when putridity has seized on the earth after excessive rains, you are to know that sensations can be begotten out of no sensations.

But if haply anyone shall say that sense so far may arise from no sensation by a process of change, or because it is brought forth by a kind of birth, it will be enough to make plain and to prove to him that no birth takes place until a union of elements has first been effected, and that nothing changes without such a process of uniting. Above all, senses cannot exist in any body before the nature itself of the living things has been begotten, because sure enough, the matter remains scattered about in air, rivers, earth and things produced from earth, and has not met together and combined in appropriate fashion the vital motions by which the all-discerning senses are kindled into action in each living thing.

Again, a blow more severe than its nature can endure prostrates at once any living thing and goes on to stun all the senses of body and mind. For the positions of the first-beginnings are broken up and the vital motions entirely stopped, until the matter, disordered by the shock through the whole frame, unties from the body the vital fastenings of the soul and scatters it abroad and forces it out through all the pores. For what more can we suppose the infliction of a blow can do, than shake from their place and break up the union of the several elements? Often too when the blow is inflicted with less violence, the remaining vital motions are wont to prevail, to prevail, I say, and still the huge disorders caused by the blow and recall each part into its proper channels and shake off the motion of death now reigning, as it were, paramount in the body and kindle afresh the almost lost senses. For in what other way should the thing be able to gather together its powers of mind and come back to life from the very threshold of death, rather than pass on to the goal to which it had almost run and so pass away?

Again, since there is pain when the bodies of matter are disordered by any force throughout the living flesh and frame and quake in their seats within, and as when they travel back into their place, a soothing pleasure ensues, you are to know that first-beginnings can be assailed by no pain and can derive no pleasure from themselves; since they are not formed of any bodies of first-beginnings, so as to be distressed by any novelty in their motion or derive from it any fruit of fostering delight; and therefore they must not be possessed of any sense.

Again, if in order that living creatures may severally have sense, sense is to be assigned to their first-beginnings as well, what are we to say of those of which mankind is specifically made? Sure enough, they both burst into fits of shaking laughter and sprinkle with dewy tears face and cheeks and have the cunning to speak at length on the nature of things and enquire next what their own first-beginnings are; since like in their natures to the entire mortals, they must in their turn be formed out of other elements, then those others out of others, so that you can venture nowhere to come to a stop; yes, whatever you shall say speaks and laughs and thinks, I will press you with the argument that it is formed of other things performing these same acts. But if we see these notions to be sheer folly and madness, and a man may laugh though not made of laughing things, and think and reason in learned language though not formed of thoughtful and eloquent seeds, why cannot the things which we see to have sense just as well be made up of a mixture of things altogether devoid of sense?

Again, we are all sprung from a heavenly seed, all have that same father by whom mother earth, the giver of increase, when she has taken in from him liquid drops of moisture, conceives and bears goodly crops and joyous trees and the race of man, bears all kinds of brute beasts, in that she supplies food with which all feed their bodies and lead a pleasant life and continue their race; wherefore with good cause she has gotten the name of mother. That also which before was from the earth passes back into the earth, and that which was sent from the borders of ether is carried back and taken in again by the quarters of heaven. Death does not extinguish things in such a way as to destroy the bodies of matter, but only breaks up the union amongst them, and then joins anew the different elements with others; and thus it comes to pass that all things change their shapes and alter their colours and receive sensations and in a moment yield them up; so that from all this you may know it matters much with what others and in what position the same first-beginnings of things are held in union and what motions they do mutually impart and receive, and you must not suppose that that which we see floating about on the surface of things and now born, then at once perishing, can be a property inherent in everlasting first bodies. Moreover, in our verses themselves it matters much with what other elements and in what kind of order the several elements are placed. If not all, yet by far the greatest number are alike; but the totals composed of them are made to differ by the position of these elements. Thus in actual things as well, when the clashings, motions, arrangement, position, shapes of matter change about, the things also must change.

Apply now, we entreat, your mind to true reason. For a new question struggles earnestly to gain your ears, a new aspect of things to display itself. But there is nothing so easy as not to be at first more difficult to believe than afterwards; and nothing too so great, so marvellous, that all do not gradually lessen their admiration of it. Look up at the bright and unsullied hue of heaven and the stars which it holds within it, wandering all about, and the moon and the sun's light of dazzling brilliancy: if all these things were now for the first time—if, I say, they were now suddenly presented to mortals beyond all expectation—what could have been named that would be more marvellous than these things, or that nations beforehand would less venture to believe could be? Nothing, methinks, so wondrous strange had been this sight. Yet how little, you know, wearied as all are to satiety with seeing, anyone now cares to look up into heaven's glittering quarters! Cease therefore to be dismayed by the mere novelty and so to reject reason from your mind with loathing: weigh the questions rather with keen judgment and if they seem to you to be true, surrender, or if the thing is false, gird yourself to the encounter. For since the sum of space is unlimited outside beyond these walls of the world, the mind seeks to apprehend what there is yonder there, to which the spirit ever yearns to look forward, and to which the mind's immission reaches in free and unembarrassed flight.

In the first place we see that round in all directions, about, above and underneath, throughout the universe there is no bound, as I have shown and as the thing of itself proclaims with loud voice and as clearly shines out in the nature of bottomless space. In no wise then can it be deemed probable, when space yawns illimitable towards all points and seeds in number numberless and sum unfathomable fly about in manifold ways driven on in ceaseless motion, that this single earth and heaven have been brought into being, that those bodies of matter so many in number do nothing outside them; the more so that this world has been made by nature, and the seeds of things chancing spontaneously to clash, after being brought together in manifold wise without purpose, without foresight, without result, have at last combined in such masses as, suddenly thrown together, became on each occasion the rudiments of great things, of earth, sea and heaven and the race of living things. Wherefore again and again, I say, you must admit that there are elsewhere other combinations of matter like to this which ether holds in its greedy grasp.

Again, when much matter is at hand, when room is there and there is no thing, no cause to hinder, things sure enough must go on and be completed. Well then, if on the one hand there is so great a store of seeds as the whole life of living creatures cannot reckon up, and if the same force and nature abide in them and have the power to throw the seeds of things together into their several places in the same way as they are thrown together into our world, you must admit that in other parts of space there are other earths and various races of men and kinds of wild beasts.

Moreover, in the sum of all there is no one thing which is begotten single in its kind and grows up single and sole of its kind; but a thing always belongs to some class and there are many other things in the same kind. First in the case of living things, most noble Memmius, you will find that in this sort has been begotten the mountain-ranging race of wild beasts, in this sort the breed of men, in this sort too the mute shoals of scaly creatures and all bodies of fowl. Wherefore on a like principle you must admit that earth and sun, moon, sea and all things else that are, are not single in their kind, but rather in number past numbering; since the deep-set boundary mark of life just as much awaits these and they are just as much of a body that had birth, as any class of things which here on earth abounds in samples of its kind.

If you well apprehend and keep in mind these things, nature, free at once and rid of her haughty lords, is seen to do all things spontaneously of herself without the meddling of the gods. For I appeal to the holy breasts of the gods who in tranquil peace pass a calm time and an unruffled existence, who can rule the sum, who hold in his hand with controlling force the strong reins of the immeasurable deep? Who can at once make all the different heavens to roll and warm with ethereal fires all the fruitful earths, or be present in all places at all times, to bring darkness with clouds and shake with noise the heaven's serene expanse, to hurl lightnings and often throw down his own temples, and withdrawing into the deserts there to spend his rage in practising his bolt which often passes the guilty by and strikes dead the innocent and unoffending?

And since the birth time of the world and first day of being, to sea and earth and the formation of the sun many bodies have been added from without, many seeds added all round, which the great universe in tossing to and fro has contributed; that from them the sea and lands might increase and from them heaven's mansion might enlarge its expanse and raise its high vaults far above earth, and that air might rise up around. For all bodies from all quarters are assigned by blows each to its appropriate thing and all withdraw to their proper classes;

moisture passes to moisture, from an earthy body earth increases and fires forge fires and ether ether, until nature, parent of things, with finishing hand has brought all things on to their utmost limit of growth. And this comes to pass when that which is infused into the life arteries is no more than that which ebbs from them and withdraws: at this point the life growth in all things must stop, at this point nature by her powers checks further increase. For whatever things you see grow in size with joyous increase and mount by successive steps to mature age, take to themselves more bodies than they discharge from themselves, while food is readily infused into all the arteries and the things are not so widely spread out as to throw off many particles and occasion more waste than their age can take in as nourishment. For no doubt it must be conceded that many bodies ebb away and withdraw from things; but still more must join them, until they have touched the utmost point of growth. Then piece by piece age breaks their powers and matured strength and wastes away on the side of decay. For the larger a thing is and the wider, as soon as its growth is stopped, at once it sheds abroad and discharges from it more bodies in all directions round; and its food is not readily transmitted into all its arteries and is not enough, in proportion to the copious exhalations which the thing throws off, to enable a like amount to rise up and be supplied. For food must keep all things entire by renewing them, food must uphold, food sustain all things: all in vain, since the arteries refuse to hold what is sufficient, and nature does not furnish the needful amount. With good reason therefore all things perish, when they have been rarefied by the ebb of particles and succumb to blows from without, since food sooner or later fails advanced age, and bodies never cease to destroy a thing by thumping it from without and to overpower it by aggressive blows. In this way then the walls too of the great world around shall be stormed and fall to decay and crumbling ruin. Yes and even now the age is enfeebled and the earth, exhausted by bearing, scarce produces little living creatures, she who produced all races and gave birth to the huge bodies of wild beasts. For methinks no golden chain let down to earth from heaven above the races of mortal beings, nor did the sea and waves which lash the rocks produce them, but the same earth bare them which now feeds them from herself. Moreover, she first spontaneously of herself produced for mortals goodly corn crops and joyous vineyards; of herself gave sweet fruits and glad pastures; which nowadays scarce attain any size when furthered by our labour: we exhaust the oxen and the strength of the husbandmen; we wear out our iron, scarce equal to the tillage of the fields; so niggardly are they of their produce and after so much labour do they let it grow. And now the aged ploughman shakes his head and sighs again and again to think that the labours of his hands have come to nothing; and when he compares present times with times past, he often praises the fortunes of his sire and harps on the theme, how the men of old comfortably supported life on a scanty plot of ground, since the allotment of land to each man was far less of yore than now. The sorrowful planter too of the exhausted and shrivelled vine impeaches the march of time and wearies heaven, and comprehends not that all things are gradually wasting away and passing to the grave, quite forspent by age and length of days.

Book Three

THEE, who first wast able amid such thick darkness to raise on high so bright a beacon and shed a light on the true interests of life, thee I follow, glory of the Greek race, and plant now my footsteps firmly fixed in thy imprinted marks, not so much from a desire to rival thee as that from the love I bear thee I yearn to imitate thee; for why need the swallow contend with swans, or what likeness is there between the feats of racing performed by kids with tottering limbs and by the powerful strength of the horse? Thou, father, art discoverer of things, thou furnishest us with fatherly precepts, and like as bees sip of all things in the flowery lawns, we, O glorious being, in like manner feed from out thy pages upon all the golden maxims, golden I say, most worthy ever of endless life. For soon as thy philosophy, issuing from a godlike intellect, has begun with loud voice to proclaim the nature of things, the terrors of the mind are dispelled, the walls of the world part asunder, I see things in operation throughout the whole void: the divinity of the gods is revealed and their tranquil abodes, which neither winds do shake nor clouds drench with rains nor snow congealed by sharp frost harms with hoary fall: an ever cloudless ether o'ercanopies them, and they laugh with light shed largely round. Nature too supplies all their wants and nothing ever impairs their peace of mind. But on the other hand, the Acherusian quarters are nowhere to be seen, though earth is no bar to all things being descried, which are in operation underneath our feet throughout the void. At all this a kind of godlike delight mixed with shuddering awe comes over me to think that nature by thy power is laid thus visibly open, is thus unveiled on every side.

And now since I have shown whatlike the beginnings of all

things are and how diverse with varied shapes as they fly spontaneously driven on in everlasting motion, and how all things
can be severally produced out of these, next after these questions the nature of the mind and soul should methinks be
cleared up by my verses and that dread of Acheron be driven
headlong forth, troubling as it does the life of man from its
inmost depths and overspreading all things with the blackness
of death, allowing no pleasure to be pure and unalloyed. For
as to what men often give out that diseases and a life of shame
are more to be feared than Tartarus, place of death, and that
they know the soul to be of blood or it may be of wind, if haply their choice so direct, and that they have no need at all of
our philosophy, you may perceive for the following reasons
that all these boasts are thrown out more for glory's sake than
because the thing is really believed. These very men, exiles
from their country and banished far from the sight of men,
live degraded by foul charge of guilt, sunk, in a word, in every
kind of misery, and whithersoever the poor wretches have
come, they yet do offer sacrifices to the dead and slaughter
black sheep and make libations to the gods' manes and in times
of distress turn their thoughts to religion much more earnestly.
Wherefore you can better test the man in doubts and dangers
and mid adversity learn who he is; for then and not till then
the words of truth are forced out from the bottom of his heart:
the mask is torn off, the reality is left. Avarice again and blind
lust of honours, which constrain unhappy men to overstep the
bounds of right and sometimes as partners and agents of
crimes to strive night and day with surpassing effort to struggle up to the summit of power—these sores of life are in no
small measure fostered by the dread of death. For foul scorn
and pinching want in every case are seen to be far removed
from a life of pleasure and security and to be a loitering, so to
say, before the gates of death. And while men driven on by an
unreal dread wish to escape far away from these and keep
them far from them, they amass wealth by civil bloodshed and
greedily double their riches, piling up murder on murder;
cruelly triumph in sad death of a brother and hate and fear
the tables of kinsfolk. Often likewise from the same fear envy
causes them to pine: they make moan that before their very
eyes he is powerful, he attracts attention, who walks arrayed
in gorgeous dignity, while they are wallowing in darkness and
dirt. Some wear themselves to death for the sake of statues

and a name. And often to such a degree through dread of death does hate of life and of the sight of daylight seize upon mortals, that they commit self-murder with a sorrowing heart, quite forgetting that this fear is the source of their cares, puts shame to rout, bursts asunder the bonds of friendship and in fine overturns duty from its very base; since often ere now men have betrayed country and dear parents in seeking to shun the Acherusian quarters. For even as children are flurried and dread all things in the thick darkness, thus we in the daylight fear at times things not a whit more to be dreaded than what children shudder at in the dark and fancy sure to be. This terror, therefore, and darkness of mind must be dispelled not by the rays of the sun and glittering shafts of day, but by the aspect and law of nature.

First then I say that the mind, which we often call the understanding, in which dwells the directing and governing principle of life, is no less part of the man than hand and foot and eyes are parts of the whole living creature. [Some, however, affirm] that the sense of the mind does not dwell in a distinct part, but is a certain vital state of the body, which the Greeks call *harmonia,* because by it, they say, we live with sense, though the understanding is in no one part; just as when good health is said to belong to the body, though yet it is not any one part of the man in health. In this way they do not assign a distinct part to the sense of the mind; in all which they appear to me to be grievously at fault in more ways than one. Oftentimes the body which is visible to sight is sick, while yet we have pleasure in another hidden part; and oftentimes the case is the very reverse, the man who is unhappy in mind feeling pleasure in his whole body; just as if, while a sick man's foot is pained, the head meanwhile should be in no pain at all. Moreover, when the limbs are consigned to soft sleep and the burdened body lies diffused without sense, there is yet a something else in us which during that time is moved in many ways and admits into it all the motions of joy and unreal cares of the heart. Now, that you may know that the soul as well is in the limbs and that the body is not wont to have sense by any harmony, this is a main proof: when much of the body has been taken away, still life often stays in the limbs; and yet the same life, when a few bodies of heat have been dispersed abroad and some air has been forced out through the mouth, abandons at once the veins and quits the bones: by this you may perceive that all bodies have not functions of like importance nor alike uphold existence, but rather that those seeds which constitute wind and heat cause life to stay in the limbs. Therefore vital heat and wind are within the body, and abandon our frame at death. Since then the nature of the mind and that of the soul have been proved to be a part, as it were, of the man, surrender the name of harmony, whether brought down to musicians from high Helicon, or whether rather they have themselves taken it from something else and transferred it to that thing which then was in need of a distinctive name; whatever it be, let them keep it: do you take in the rest of my precepts.

Now I assert that the mind and the soul are kept together in close union and make up a single nature, but that the directing principle, which we call mind and understanding, is the head, so to speak, and reigns paramount in the whole body. It has a fixed seat in the middle region of the breast: here throb fear and apprehension, about these spots dwell soothing joys; therefore here is the understanding or mind. All the rest of the soul disseminated through the whole body obeys and moves at will and inclination of the mind. It by itself alone knows for itself, rejoices for itself, at times when the impression does not move either soul or body together with it. And as when some part of us, the head or the eye, suffers from an attack of pain, we do not feel the anguish at the same time over the whole body, thus the mind sometimes suffers pain by itself or is inspirited with joy, when all the rest of the soul throughout the limbs and frame is stirred by no novel sensation. But when the mind is excited by some more vehement apprehension, we see the whole soul feel in unison through all the limbs, and thus sweats and paleness spread over the whole body, the tongue falter, the voice die away, a mist cover the eyes, the ears ring, the limbs sink under one; in short, we often see men drop down from terror of mind; so that anybody may easily perceive from this that the soul is closely united with the mind, and when it has been smitten by the influence of the mind, forthwith pushes and strikes the body.

This same principle teaches that the nature of the mind and soul is bodily; for when it is seen to push the limbs, rouse the body from sleep, and alter the countenance and guide and turn about the whole man, and when we see that none of these effects can take place without touch nor touch without body, must we not admit that the mind and the soul are of a bodily nature? Again you perceive that our mind in our body suffers together with the body and feels in unison with it. When a weapon with a shudder-causing force has been driven in and has laid bare bones and sinews within the body, if it does not take life, yet there ensues a faintness and a lazy sinking to the ground and on the ground the turmoil of mind which arises, and sometimes a kind of undecided inclination to get up. Therefore the nature of the mind must be bodily, since it suffers from bodily weapons and blows.

I will now go on to explain in my verses of what kind of body the mind consists and out of what it has been formed. First of all I say that it is extremely fine and formed of exceedingly minute bodies. That this is so you may, if you please to attend, clearly perceive from what follows: nothing that is seen takes place with a velocity equal to that of the mind when it starts some suggestion and actually sets it agoing; the mind therefore is stirred with greater rapidity than any of the things whose nature stands out visible to sight. But that which is so passing nimble must consist of seeds exceedingly round and exceedingly minute, in order to be stirred and set in motion by a small moving power. Thus water is moved and heaves by ever so small a force, formed as it is of small particles apt to roll. But on the other hand, the nature of honey is more sticky, its liquid more sluggish and its movement more dilatory; for the whole mass of matter coheres more closely, because, sure enough, it is made of bodies not so smooth, fine and round. A breeze, however gentle and light, can force, as you may see, a high heap of poppy seed to be blown away from the top downwards; but on the other hand, Eurus itself cannot move a heap of stones. Therefore bodies possess a power of moving in proportion to their smallness and smoothness; and on the other hand, the greater weight and roughness bodies prove to have, the more stable they are. Since then the nature of the mind has been found to be eminently easy to move, it must consist of bodies exceedingly small, smooth and round. The knowledge of which fact, my good friend, will on many accounts prove useful and be serviceable to you. The following fact too likewise demonstrates how fine the texture is of which its nature is composed, and how small the room is in which it can be contained, could it only be collected into one mass: soon as the untroubled sleep of death has gotten hold of a man and the nature of the mind and soul has withdrawn, you can perceive then no diminution of the entire body either in appearance or weight: death makes all good save the vital sense and heat. Therefore the whole soul must consist of very small seeds and be inwoven through veins, flesh, sinews; inasmuch as, after it has all withdrawn from the whole body, the exterior contour of the limbs preserves itself entire and not a tittle of the weight is lost. Just in the same way, when the flavour of wine is gone or when the delicious aroma of a perfume has been dispersed into the air or when the savour has left some body, yet the thing itself does not therefore look smaller to the eye, nor does aught seem to have been taken from the weight, because, sure enough, many minute seeds make up the savours and the odour in the whole body of the several things. Therefore, again and again I say, you are to know that the nature of the mind and the soul has been formed of exceedingly minute seeds, since at its departure it takes away none of the weight.

We are not, however, to suppose that this nature is single. For a certain subtle spirit mixed with heat quits men at death, and then the heat draws air along with it; there being no heat which has not air too mixed with it: for since its nature is rare, many first-beginnings of air must move about through it. Thus then the nature of the mind is proved to be threefold; and yet these things all together ⁓re not sufficient to produce sense; since the fact of the case does not admit that any of these can produce sense-giving motions and the thoughts which a man turns over in mind. Thus some fourth nature too must be added to these: it is altogether without name; than it nothing exists more nimble or more fine, or of smaller or smoother elements: it first transmits the sense-giving motions through the frame; for it is first stirred, made up as it is of small particles; next the heat and the unseen force of the spirit receives the motions, then the air; then all things are set in action, the blood is stirred, every part of the flesh is filled with sensation; last of all the feeling is transmitted to the bones and marrow, whether it be one of pleasure or an opposite excitement. No pain, however, can lightly pierce thus far nor any sharp malady make its way in, without all things being so thoroughly disordered that no room is left for life and the parts of the soul fly abroad through all the pores of the body. But commonly a stop is put to these motions on the surface, as it were, of the body: for this reason we are able to retain life.

Now though I would fain explain in what way these are

mixed up together and what is the method of their arrangement when they exert their powers, the poverty of my native
speech deters me sorely against my will; yet will I touch upon
them and in summary fashion to the best of my ability: the
first-beginnings of their mutual motions are interlaced in such
a way that none of them can be separated by itself, nor can
the function of any go on divided from the rest of any interval;
but they are, so to say, the several qualities of one body. Even
so, in any flesh of living creature you please, without exception there is a smell and a heat and savour, and yet out of all
these is made up one single bulk of body. Thus the heart and
the air and the unseen power of the spirit mixed together produce a single nature, together with that nimble force which
transmits to them from itself the origin of motion; by which
means sense-giving motion first takes its rise through the flesh-
ly frame. For this nature lurks secreted in its inmost depths,
and nothing in our body is farther beneath all ken than it, and
more than this, it is the very soul of the whole soul. Just in the
same way as the power of the mind and the function of the
soul are latent in our limbs and throughout our body, because
they are each formed of small and few bodies: even so, you
are to know, this nameless power made of minute bodies is
concealed and is, moreover, the very soul, so to say, of the
whole soul, and reigns supreme in the whole body. On a like
principle the spirit and air and heat must, as they exert their
powers, be mixed up together through the frame, and one
must ever be more out of view or more prominent than another, that a single substance may be seen to be formed from
the union of all, lest the heat and spirit apart by themselves
and the power of the air apart by itself should destroy sense
and dissipate it by their disunion. Thus the mind possesses
that heat which it displays when it boils up in anger and fire
flashes from the keen eyes; there is too much cold spirit, com-
rade of fear, which spreads a shivering over the limbs and stirs
the whole frame; yes and there is also that condition of still air
which has place when the breast is calm and the looks cheer-
ful. But they have more of the hot whose keen heart and passionate mind lightly boil up in anger. Foremost in this class
comes the fierce violence of lions, who often as they chafe
break their hearts with their roaring and cannot contain within their breast the billows of their rage. Then the chilly mind
of stags is fuller of the spirit and more quickly rouses through

all the flesh its icy currents, which cause a shivering motion to pass over the limbs. But the nature of oxen has its life rather from the still air, and never does the smoky torch of anger applied to it stimulate it too much, shedding over it the shadow of murky gloom, nor is it transfixed and stiffened by the icy shafts of fear: it lies between the other two, stags and cruel lions. And thus it is with mankind: however much teaching renders some equally refined, it yet leaves behind the earliest traces of the nature of each mind; and we are not to suppose that evil habits can be so thoroughly plucked up by the roots, that one man shall not be more prone than another to keen anger, a second shall not be somewhat more quickly assailed by fear, a third shall not take some things more meekly than is right. In many other points there must be differences between the varied natures of men and the tempers which follow upon these; though at present I am unable to set forth the hidden causes of these or to find names enough for the different shapes which belong to the first-beginnings, from which shapes arises this diversity of things. What herein I think I may affirm is this: traces of the different natures left behind, which reason is unable to expel from us, are so exceedingly slight that there is nothing to hinder us from living a life worthy of gods.

Well, this nature is contained by the whole body and is in turn the body's guardian and the cause of its existence; for the two adhere together with common roots and cannot, it is plain, be riven asunder without destruction. Even as it is not easy to pluck the perfume out of lumps of frankincense without quite destroying its nature as well; so it is not easy to withdraw from the whole body the nature of the mind and soul without dissolving all alike. With first-beginnings so interlaced from their earliest birth are they formed and gifted with a life of joint partnership, and it is plain that the faculty of the body and of the mind cannot feel separately, each alone without the other's power, but sense is kindled throughout our flesh and blown into flame between the two by the joint motions on the part of both. Moreover, the body by itself is never either begotten or grows or, it is plain, continues to exist after death. For not in the way that the liquid of water often loses the heat which has been given to it, yet is not for that reason itself riven in pieces, but remains unimpaired—not in this way, I say, can the abandoned frame endure the separation of the soul, but riven in pieces it utterly perishes and rots away. Thus the mutual connexions of body and soul from the first moment of their existence learn the vital motions even while hid in the body and womb of the mother, so that no separation can take place without mischief and ruin. Thus you may see that, since the cause of existence lies in their joint action, their nature too must be a joint nature.

Furthermore, if anyone tries to disprove that the body feels and believes that the soul mixed through the whole body takes upon it this motion which we name sense, he combats even manifest and undoubted facts. For who will ever bring forward any explanation of what the body's feeling is, except that which the plain fact of the case has itself given and taught to us? But when the soul, it is said, has departed, the body throughout is without sense; yes, for it loses what was not its own peculiar property in life.

Again, to say that the eyes can see no object, but that the soul discerns through them as through an open door, is far from easy, since their sense contradicts this; and the more so that often we are unable to perceive shining things, because our eyes are embarrassed by the lights. But this is not the case with doors; for, because we ourselves see, the open doors do not therefore undergo any fatigue. Again, if our eyes are in the place of doors, in that case when the eyes are removed, the mind ought, it would seem, to have more power of seeing things after doors, jambs and all, have been taken out of the way.

And herein you must by no means adopt the opinion which the revered judgment of the worthy man Democritus lays down, that the first-beginnings of body and mind placed together in successive layers come in alternate order and so weave the tissue of our limbs. For not only are the elements of the soul much smaller than those of which our body and flesh are formed, but they are also much fewer in number and are disseminated merely in scanty number through the frame, so that you can warrant no more than this: the first-beginnings of the soul keep spaces between them at least as great as are the smallest bodies which, if thrown upon it, are first able to excite in our body the sense-giving motions. Thus at times we do not feel the adhesion of dust when it settles on our body, nor the impact of chalk when it rests on our limbs, nor do we feel a mist at night nor a spider's slender threads as they come against us, when we are caught in its meshes in moving along, nor the same insect's flimsy web when it has fallen on our head, nor the feathers of birds and down of plants as it flies about, which commonly from exceeding lightness does not lightly fall, nor do we feel the tread of every creeping creature whatsoever nor each particular footprint which gnats and the like stamp on our body. So invariably must many seeds mixed up in our bodies throughout our frames be set in motion ere the first-beginnings of the soul are roused to feel, and ere by thumping with such spaces between they can clash, unite and in turn recoil.

The mind has more to do with holding the fastnesses of life and has more sovereign sway over it than the power of the soul. For without the understanding and the mind, no part of the soul can maintain itself in the frame the smallest fraction of time, but follows at once in the other's train and passes away into the air and leaves the cold limbs in the chill of death. But he abides in life whose mind and understanding continue to stay with him: though the trunk is mangled with its limbs shorn all round about it, after the soul has been taken away on all sides and been severed from the limbs, the trunk yet lives and inhales the ethereal airs of life. When robbed, if not of the whole, yet of a large portion of the soul, it still lingers in and cleaves to life; just as, after the eye has been lacerated all round, if the pupil has continued uninjured, the living power of sight remains, provided always you do not destroy the whole ball of the eye and pare close round the pupil and leave only it; for that will not be done without destroying the eyes. But if that middle portion of the eye, small as it is, is eaten into, the sight is gone at once and darkness ensues, though a man have the bright ball quite unimpaired. On such terms of union soul and mind are ever bound to each other.

Now mark me: that you may know that the minds and light souls of living creatures have birth and are mortal, I will go on to set forth verses worthy of your attention got together by long study and invented with welcome effort. Do you mind to attach to either of the two either name, and when for instance I shall choose to speak of the soul, showing it to be mortal, believe that I speak of the mind as well, inasmuch as both make up one thing and are one united substance. First of all then, since I have shown the soul to be fine and to be formed of minute bodies and made up of much smaller first-beginnings than is the liquid of water or mist or smoke—for it far surpasses these in nimbleness and is moved if struck by a far slenderer cause; inasmuch as it is moved by images of smoke and mist; as when, for instance, sunk in sleep we see altars steam forth their heat and send up their smoke on high; for beyond a doubt images are begotten for us from these things —well then, since you see on the vessels being shattered the water flow away on all sides, and since mist and smoke pass away into air, believe that the soul too is shed abroad and perishes much more quickly and dissolves sooner into its first bodies, when once it has been taken out of the limbs of man and has withdrawn. For how can you believe that this soul, which the body that serves for its vessel cannot hold, if shattered from any cause and rarefied by the withdrawal of blood from the veins, how can you believe, I say, that this soul can be held by any air? How can that air which is rarer than our body hold it in?

Again, we perceive that the mind is begotten along with the body and grows up together with it and becomes old along with it. For even as children go about with a tottering and weakly body, so slender sagacity of mind follows along with it; then when their life has reached the maturity of confirmed strength, the judgment too is greater and the power of the mind more developed. Afterwards, when the body has been shattered by the mastering might of time and the frame has drooped with its forces dulled, then the intellect halts, the tongue dotes, the mind gives way, all faculties fail and are found wanting at the same time. It naturally follows then that the whole nature of the soul is dissolved, like smoke, into the high air; since we see it is begotten along with the body and grows up along with it and, as I have shown, breaks down at the same time, worn out with age.

Moreover, we see that even as the body is liable to violent diseases and severe pain, so is the mind to sharp cares and grief and fear; it naturally follows therefore that it is its partner in death as well. Again, in diseases of the body the mind often wanders and goes astray; for it loses its reason and drivels in its speech and often in a profound lethargy is carried into deep and never-ending sleep with drooping eyes and head; out of which it neither hears the voices nor can recognise the faces of those who stand round calling it back to life and bedewing with tears face and cheeks. Therefore you must admit that the mind too dissolves, since the infection of disease reaches to it; for the pain and disease are both forgers of death: a truth we have fully learned ere now by the death of many. Again, when the pungent strength of wine has entered into a man and its spirit has been infused into and transmitted through his veins, why is it that a heaviness of the limbs follows along with this, his legs are hampered as he reels about, his tongue falters, his mind is besotted, his eyes swim, shouting, hiccuping, wranglings are rife, together with all the other usual concomitants—why is all this, if not because the overpowering violence of the wine is wont to disorder the soul within the body? But whenever things can be disordered and hampered, they give token that if a somewhat more potent cause gained an entrance, they would perish and be robbed of all further existence. Moreover, it often happens that someone constrained by the violence of disease suddenly drops down before our eyes, as by a stroke of lightning, and foams at the mouth, moans and shivers through his frame, loses his reason, stiffens his muscles, is racked, gasps for breath fitfully, and wearies his limbs with tossing. Sure enough, because the violence of the disease spreads itself through his frame and disorders him, he foams as he tries to eject his soul, just as in the salt sea the waters boil with the mastering might of the winds. A moan too is forced out, because the limbs are seized with pain, and mainly because seeds of voice are driven forth and are carried in a close mass out by the mouth, the road which they are accustomed to take and where they have a well-paved way. Loss of reason follows, because the powers of the mind and soul are disordered and, as I have shown, are riven and forced asunder, torn to pieces by the same baneful malady. Then after the cause of the disease has bent its course back and the acrid humours of the distempered body return to their hiding places, then he first gets up like one reeling, and by little and little comes back into full possession of his senses and regains his soul. Since therefore, even within the body, mind and soul are harassed by such violent distempers and so miserably racked by sufferings, why believe that they without the body in the open air can continue existence battling with fierce winds? And since we perceive that the mind is healed like the sick body, and we see that it can be altered by medicine, this too gives warning that the mind has a mortal existence. For it is natural that whosoever essays and attempts to change the mind or seeks to alter any other nature you like, should add new parts or change the arrangement of the present, or at least withdraw some small fraction from the whole sum. But that which is immortal wills not to have its parts transposed nor any addition to be made nor one tittle to ebb away; for whenever a thing changes and quits its proper limits, this change is at once the death of that which was before. Therefore the mind, whether it is sick or whether it is altered by medicine, alike, as I have shown, gives forth mortal symptoms. So invariably is truth found to make head against false reason and to cut off all retreat from the assailant and by a two-edged refutation to put falsehood to rout.

Again, we often see a man pass gradually away and limb by limb lose vital sense; first the toes of his feet and the nails turn livid, then the feet and shanks die, then next the steps of chilly death creep with slow pace over the other members. Since in this way the nature of the soul is rent and passes away and comes not forth all at once in its entireness, it must be reckoned mortal. But if haply you suppose that it can draw itself in through the whole frame and mass its parts together and in this way withdraw sense from all the limbs, yet then the spot into which so great a store of soul is gathered ought to show itself in possession of a greater amount of sense. But as this is nowhere found, sure enough, as we said before, it is torn in pieces and scattered abroad, and therefore dies. Moreover, if I were pleased for the moment to grant what is false and admit that the soul might be collected in one mass in the body of those who leave the light dying piecemeal, even then you must admit the soul to be mortal; and it makes no difference whether it perish dispersed in air or, gathered into one lump out of all its parts, lose all feeling, since sense ever more and more fails the whole man throughout and less and less of life remains throughout.

And since the mind is one part of a man which remains fixed in a particular spot, just as are the ears and eyes and the other senses which guide and direct life; and just as the hand or eye or nose when separated from us cannot feel and exist apart, but in however short a time wastes away in putrefaction, thus the mind cannot exist by itself without the body and the man's self, which, as you see, serves for the mind's vessel or anything else you choose to imagine which implies a yet closer union with it, since the body is attached to it by the nearest ties.

Again, the quickened powers of body and mind by their joint partnership enjoy health and life; for the nature of the mind cannot by itself alone without the body give forth vital motions nor can the body, again, bereft of the soul continue to exist and make use of its senses: just, you are to know, as the eye itself torn away from its roots cannot see anything when apart from the whole body thus the soul and mind cannot, it is plain, do anything by themselves. Sure enough, because mixed up through veins and flesh, sinews and bones, their first-beginnings are confined by all the body and are not free to bound away, leaving great spaces between, therefore, thus shut in, they make those sense-giving motions which they cannot make after death when forced out of the body into the air, by reason that they are not then confined in a like manner; for the air will be a body and a living thing, if the soul shall be able to keep itself together and to enclose in it those motions which it used before to perform in the sinews and within the body. Therefore, again and again I say, when the enveloping body has been all broken up and the vital airs have been forced out, you must admit that the senses of the mind and the soul are dissolved, since the cause of destruction is one and inseparable for both body and soul.

Again, since the body is unable to bear the separation of the soul without rotting away in a noisome stench, why doubt that the power of the soul gathering itself up from the inmost depths of the body has oozed out and dispersed like smoke, and that the crumbling body has changed and tumbled in with so total a ruin for this reason, because its foundations throughout are stirred from their places, the soul oozing out abroad through the frame, through all the winding passages which are in the body, and all openings? So that in ways manifold you may learn that the nature of the soul has been divided piecemeal and gone forth throughout the frame, and that it has been first torn to shreds within the body, ere it glided forth and swam out into the air. Moreover, even while it yet moves within the confines of life, often the soul, shaken from some cause or other, is seen to wish to pass out and be loosed from the whole body, the features are seen to droop as at the last hour and all the limbs to sink flaccid over the bloodless trunk: just as happens, when, as the phrase goes, the mind is in a bad way, or the soul is quite gone; when all is hurry and everyone is anxious to keep from parting the last tie of life;

for then the mind and the power of the soul are shaken throughout and both are quite loosened together with the body; so that a cause somewhat more powerful can quite break them up. Why doubt I would ask that the soul when driven forth out of the body, when in the open air, feeble as it is, stript of its covering, not only cannot continue through eternity, but is unable to hold together the smallest fraction of time? No one when dying appears to feel the soul go forth entire from his whole body or first mount up to the throat and gullet, but all feel it fail in that part which lies in a particular quarter; just as they know that other senses suffer dissolution each in its own place. But if our mind were immortal, it would not when dying complain so much of its dissolution, as of passing abroad and quitting its vesture, like a snake.

Again, why are the mind's understanding and judgment never begotten in the head or feet or hands, but cling to one spot and fixed quarter of the man, if it be not that particular places are assigned for the birth of each part, and for the abode of each after it is born, that thus the members may be distributed with such a manifold organisation of parts, that no perverted arrangement of them shall ever show itself? So invariably effect follows cause, nor is flame wont to be born in rivers nor cold in fire.

Again, if the nature of the soul is immortal and can feel when separated from our body, methinks we must suppose it to be provided with five senses; and in no other way can we picture to ourselves souls below flitting about Acheron. Painters therefore and former generations of writers have thus represented souls provided with senses. But neither eyes nor nose nor hand can exist for the soul apart from the body nor can tongue, nor can ears perceive by the sense of hearing or exist for the soul by themselves apart from the body.

And since we perceive that vital sense is in the whole body and we see that it is all endowed with life, if on a sudden any force with swift blow shall have cut it in twain so as quite to dissever the two halves, the power of the soul will without doubt at the same time be cleft and cut asunder and dashed in twain together with the body. But that which is cut and divides into any parts, you are to know, disclaims for itself an everlasting nature. Stories are told how scythed chariots reeking with indiscriminate slaughter often lop off limbs so instantaneously that that which has fallen down lopped off from the frame is seen to quiver on the ground, while yet the mind and faculty of the man from the suddenness of the mischief cannot feel the pain; and because his mind once for all is wholly given to the business of fighting, with what remains of his body he mingles in the fray and carnage, and often perceives not that the wheels and devouring scythes have carried off among the horses' feet his left arm, shield and all; another sees not that his right arm has dropped from him, while he mounts and presses forward. Another tries to get up after he has lost his leg, while the dying foot quivers with its toes on the ground close by. The head too when cut off from the warm living trunk retains on the ground the expression of life and open eyes, until it has yielded up all the remnants of soul. To take another case, if as a serpent's tongue is quivering, as its tail is darting out from its long body, you choose to chop with an axe into many pieces both tail and body, you will see all the separate portions thus cut off writhing under the fresh wound and bespattering the earth with gore, the fore part with the mouth making for its own hinder part, to allay with burning bite the pain of the wound with which it has been smitten. Shall we say then that there are entire souls in all those pieces? Why, from that argument it will follow that one living creature had many souls in its body; and this being absurd, therefore the soul, which was one, has been divided together with the body; therefore each alike must be reckoned mortal, since each is alike chopped up into many pieces.

Again, if the nature of the soul is immortal and makes its way into our body at the time of birth, why are we unable to remember besides the time already gone, and why do we retain no traces of past actions? If the power of the mind has been so completely changed that all remembrance of past things is lost, that, methinks, differs not widely from death; therefore you must admit that the soul which was before has perished and that which now is has now been formed.

Again, if the quickened power of the mind is wont to be put into us after our body is fully formed, at the instant of our birth and our crossing the threshold of life, it ought agreeably to this to live not in such a way as to seem to have grown with the body and together with its members within the blood, but as in a den apart by and to itself: the very

contrary to what undoubted fact teaches; for it is so closely
united with the body throughout the veins, flesh, sinews and
bones, that the very teeth have a share of sense; as the act of
biting proves and the sharp twinge of cold water and the
crunching of a rough stone, when it has got into them out of
bread. Wherefore, again and again I say, we must believe
souls to be neither without a birth nor exempted from the law
of death; for we must not believe that they could have been
so completely united with our bodies, if they found their way
into them from without, nor, since they are so closely inwoven
with them, does it appear that they can get out unharmed
and unloose themselves unscathed from all the sinews and
bones and joints. But if haply you believe that the soul finds
its way in from without and is wont to ooze through all our
limbs, so much the more it will perish thus blended with the
body; for what oozes through another is dissolved, and therefore dies. As food distributed through all the cavities of the
body, while it is transmitted into the limbs and the whole
frame, is destroyed and furnishes out of itself the matter of
another nature, thus the soul and mind, though they pass
entire into a fresh body, yet in oozing through it are dissolved,
whilst there are transmitted, so to say, into the frame through
all the cavities those particles of which this nature of mind is
formed, which now is sovereign in our body, being born out
of that soul which then perished when dispersed through the
frame. Wherefore the nature of the soul is seen to be neither
without a birthday nor exempt from death.

Again, are seeds of the soul left in the dead body or not? If
they are left and remain in it, the soul cannot fairly be
deemed immortal, since it has withdrawn lessened by the loss
of some parts; but if when taken away it has fled forth with
its members so entire that it has left in the body no parts of
itself, whence do carcases exude worms from the now rank
flesh and whence does such a swarm of living things, boneless
and bloodless, surge through the heaving frame? But if
haply you believe that souls find their way into worms from
without and can severally pass each into a body and you make
no account of why many thousands of souls meet together in
a place from which one has withdrawn, this question at least
must, it seems, be raised and brought to a decisive test:
whether souls hunt out the several seeds of worms and build
for themselves a place to dwell in, or find their way into

bodies fully formed, so to say. But why they should on their part make a body or take such trouble cannot be explained; since, being without a body, they are not plagued as they flit about with diseases and cold and hunger: the body indeed is more akin to, more troubled by such infirmities, and by its contact with it the mind suffers many ills. Nevertheless, be it ever so expedient for them to make a body, when they are going to enter, yet clearly there is no way by which they can so do. Therefore souls do not make for themselves bodies and limbs; no, nor can they by any method find their way into bodies after they are fully formed; for they will neither be able to unite themselves with a nice precision nor will any connexion of mutual sensation be formed between them.

Again, why does untamed fierceness go along with the sullen brood of lions, cunning with foxes and proneness to flight with stags? And to take any other instance of the kind, why are all qualities engendered in the limbs and temper from the very commencement of life, if not because a fixed power of mind derived from its proper seed and breed grows up together with the whole body? If it were immortal and wont to pass into different bodies, living creatures would be of interchangeable dispositions; a dog of Hyrcanian breed would often fly before the attack of an antlered stag, a hawk would cower in midair as it fled at the approach of a dove, men would be without reason, the savage races of wild beasts would have reason. For the assertion that an immortal soul is altered by a change of body is advanced on a false principle. What is changed is dissolved, and therefore dies: the parts are transposed and quit their former order; therefore they must admit of being dissolved too throughout the frame, in order at last to die one and all together with the body. But if they shall say that souls of men always go into human bodies, I yet will ask how it is a soul can change from wise to foolish, and no child has discretion, and why the mare's foal is not so well trained as the powerful strength of the horse. You may be sure they will fly to the subterfuge that the mind grows weakly in a weakly body. But granting this is so, you must admit the soul to be mortal, since changed so completely throughout the frame, it loses its former life and sense. Then too, in what way will it be able to grow in strength uniformly with its allotted body and reach the coveted flower of age, unless it shall be its partner at its first beginning? Or what means it by passing out from the limbs when decayed with age? Does it fear to remain shut up in a crumbling body, fear that its tenement, worn out by protracted length of days, bury it in its ruins? Why, an immortal being incurs no risks.

Again, for souls to stand by at the unions of Venus and the birth throes of beasts seems to be passing absurd, for them, the immortals, to wait for mortal limbs in number numberless and struggle with one another in forward rivalry, which shall first and by preference have entrance in; unless haply bargains are struck among the souls on these terms, that whichever in its flight shall first come up, shall first have right of entry, and that they shall make no trial at all of each other's strength.

Again, a tree cannot exist in the ether, nor clouds in the deep sea, nor can fishes live in the fields nor blood exist in woods nor sap in stones. Where each thing can grow and abide is fixed and ordained. Thus the nature of the mind cannot come into being alone without the body nor exist far away from the sinews and blood. But if (for this would be much more likely to happen than that) the force itself of the mind might be in the head or shoulders or heels or might be born in any other part of the body, it would after all be wont to abide in one and the same man or vessel. But since in our body even it is fixed and seen to be ordained where the soul and the mind can severally be and grow, it must still more strenuously be denied that it can abide and be born out of the body altogether. Therefore when the body has died, we must admit that the soul has perished, wrenched away throughout the body. To link forsooth a mortal thing with an everlasting and suppose that they can have sense in common and can be reciprocally acted upon, is sheer folly; for what can be conceived more incongruous, more discordant and inconsistent with itself, than a thing which is mortal, linked with an immortal and everlasting thing, trying in such union to weather furious storms? But if haply the soul is to be accounted immortal for this reason rather, because it is kept sheltered from death-bringing things, either because things hostile to its existence do not approach at all, or because those which do approach in some way or other retreat discomfited before we can feel the harm they do, [manifest experience proves that this cannot be true]. For besides that it sickens in sympathy with the maladies of the body, it is often attacked by that which frets it on the score of the future and keeps it on the rack of suspense and wears it out with cares, remorse for sins gnawing it on account of past misdeeds: then there is madness peculiar to the mind and forgetfulness of all things; then too it often sinks into the black waters of lethargy.

Death therefore to us is nothing, concerns us not a jot, since the nature of the mind is proved to be mortal. And as in time gone by we felt no distress, when the Poeni from all sides came together to do battle, and all things shaken by war's troublous uproar shuddered and quaked beneath high heaven, and mortal men were in doubt which of the two peoples it should be to whose empire all must fall by sea and land alike, thus when we shall be no more, when there shall have been a separation of body and soul, out of both of which we are each formed into a single being, to us, you may be sure, who then shall be no more, nothing whatever can happen to excite sensation, not if earth shall be mingled with sea and sea with heaven. And even supposing the nature of the mind and power of the soul do feel, after they have been severed from our body, yet that is nothing to us who by the binding tie of marriage between body and soul are formed each into one single being. And if time should gather up our matter after our death and bring it once more into the condition in which it now is, and the light of life be given to us again, this result even would concern us not at all, when the chain of our self-consciousness has once been snapped asunder. So now we give ourself no concern about any self which we have been before, nor do we feel any distress on the score of that self. For when you look back on the whole past course of immeasurable time and think how manifold are the shapes which the motions of matter take, you may easily credit this too, that these very same seeds of which we now are formed have often before been placed in the same order in which they now are; and yet we cannot recover this in memory: a break in our existence has been interposed, and all the motions have wandered to and fro far astray from the sensations they produced. For he whom evil is to befall must in his own person exist at the very time it comes, if the misery and suffering are haply to have any place at all; but since death precludes this, and forbids him to be, upon whom the ills can be brought, you may be sure that we have nothing to fear after death, and that he who exists not, cannot become miserable, and that it matters not a whit whether he has been born into life at any other time, when immortal death has taken away his mortal life.

Therefore when you see a man bemoaning his hard case, that after death he shall either rot with his body laid in the grave or be devoured by flames or the jaws of wild beasts, you may be sure that his ring betrays a flaw and that there lurks in his heart a secret goad, though he himself declare that he does not believe that any sense will remain to him after death. He does not, methinks, really grant the conclusion which he professes to grant nor the principle on which he so professes, nor does he take and force himself root and branch out of life, but all unconsciously imagines something of self to survive. For when anyone in life suggests to himself that birds and beasts will rend his body after death, he makes moan for himself: he does not separate himself from that self, nor withdraw himself fully from the body so thrown out, and fancies himself that other self and stands by and impregnates it with his own sense. Hence he makes much moan that he has been born mortal, and sees not that after real death there will be no other self to remain in life and lament to self that his own self has met death, and there to stand and grieve that his own self there lying is mangled or burnt. For if it is an evil after death to be pulled about by the devouring jaws of wild beasts, I cannot see why it should not be a cruel pain to be laid on fires and burn in hot flames, or to be placed in honey and stifled, or to stiffen with cold, stretched on the smooth surface of an icy slab of stone, or to be pressed down and crushed by a load of earth above.

"Now no more shall thy house admit thee with glad welcome, nor a most virtuous wife and sweet children run to be the first to snatch kisses and touch thy heart with a silent joy. No more mayst thou be prosperous in thy doings, a safeguard to thine own. One disastrous day has taken from thee, luckless man, in luckless wise all the many prizes of life." This do men say; but add not thereto, "and now no longer does any craving for these things beset thee withal." For if they could rightly perceive this in thought and follow up the thought in words, they would release themselves from great distress and apprehension of mind. "Thou, even as now thou art, sunk in the sleep of death, shalt continue so to be all time to come, freed from all distressful pains; but we with a sorrow that would not be sated wept for thee, when close by thou didst turn to an ashen hue on thy appalling funeral pile, and no length of days shall pluck from our hearts our ever-during grief." This question therefore should be asked of this speaker, what there is in it so passing bitter, if it come in the end to sleep and rest, that anyone should pine in never-ending sorrow.

This too men often, when they have reclined at table, cup in hand, and shade their brows with crowns, love to say from the heart: "Short is this enjoyment for poor weak men; presently it will have been and never after may it be called back." As if after their death it is to be one of their chiefest afflictions that thirst and parching drought is to burn them up hapless wretches, or a craving for anything else is to beset them. What folly! No one feels the want of himself and life at the time when mind and body are together sunk in sleep; for all we care this sleep might be everlasting, no craving whatever for ourselves then moves us. And yet by no means do those first-beginnings throughout our frame wander at that time far away from their sense-producing motions, when a man starts up from sleep and collects himself at once. Death therefore must be thought to concern us much less, if less there can be than what we see to be nothing; for a greater dispersion of the mass of matter follows in the train of death, and no one wakes up, upon whom the chill cessation of life has once come.

Once more, if the nature of things could suddenly utter a voice and in person could rally any of us in such words as these: "What hast thou, O mortal, so much at heart, that thou goest such lengths in sickly sorrows? Why bemoan and bewail death? For say thy life past and gone has been welcome to thee and thy blessings have not all, as if they were poured into a perforated vessel, run through and been lost without avail: why not then take thy departure like a guest filled with life, and with resignation, thou fool, enter upon untroubled rest? But if all that thou hast enjoyed has been squandered and lost and life is a grievance, why seek to make any addition, to be wasted perversely in its turn and lost utterly without avail? Why not rather make an end of life and travail? For there is nothing more which I can contrive and discover for thee to give pleasure: all things are ever the same. Though thy body is not yet decayed with years nor thy frame worn out and exhausted, yet all things remain the same, ay, though in length of life thou shouldst outlast all races of things now living, nay, even more if thou shouldst never die," what answer have we to make save this, that nature sets up against us a well-founded claim and puts forth in her pleading a true indictment? If, however, one of greater age and more advanced in years should complain and lament, poor wretch, his death more than is right, would she not with greater cause raise her voice and rally him in sharp accents: "Away from this time forth with thy tears, rascal; a truce to thy complainings: thou decayest after full enjoyment of all the prizes of life. But because thou ever yearnest for what is not present, and despisest what is, life has slipped from thy grasp unfinished and unsatisfying, and or ever thou thoughtest, death has taken his stand at thy pillow, before thou canst take thy departure sated and filled with good things. Now, however, give up all things unsuited to thy age, and come and with a good grace rather take thyself off; for it must be so." With good reason, methinks, she would bring her charge, with reason rally and reproach; for old things give way and are supplanted by new without fail, and one thing must ever be replenished out of other things; and no one is delivered over to the pit and black Tartarus: matter is needed for after generations to grow; all of which, though, will follow thee when they have finished their term of life; and thus it is that all these no less than thou have before this come to an end and hereafter will come to an end. Thus one thing will never cease to rise out of another, and life is granted to none in fee-simple, to all in usufruct. Think too how the bygone antiquity of everlasting time before our birth was nothing to us. Nature therefore holds this up to us as a mirror of the time yet to come after our death. Is there aught in this that looks appalling, aught that wears an aspect of gloom? Is it not more untroubled than any sleep?

And those things, sure enough, which are fabled to be in the deep of Acheron, do all exist for us in this life. No Tantalus, numbed by groundless terror, as the story is, fears, poor wretch, a huge stone hanging in air; but in life rather a baseless dread of the gods vexes mortals: the fall they fear is such fall of luck as chance brings to each. Nor do birds eat a way into Tityus, laid in Acheron, nor can they, sooth to say, find during eternity food to peck under his large breast. However huge the bulk of body he extends, though such as to take up with outspread limbs not nine acres merely, but the whole earth, yet will he not be able to endure everlasting pain and supply food from his own body forever. But he is for us a Tityus whom, as he grovels in love, vultures rend and bitter, bitter anguish eats up or troubled thoughts from any other passion do rive. In life too we have a Sisyphus before our eyes who is bent on asking from the people the rods and cruel axes, and always retires defeated and disappointed. For to ask for power, which empty as it is is never given, and always in the chase of it to undergo severe toil, this is forcing up-hill with much effort a stone which after all rolls back again from the summit and seeks in headlong haste the levels of the plain. Then to be ever feeding the thankless nature of the mind, and never to fill it full and sate it with good things, as the seasons of the year do for us, when they come round and bring their fruits and varied delights, though after all we are never filled with the enjoyments of life, this, methinks, is to do what is told of the maidens in the flower of their age, to keep pouring water into a perforated vessel which in spite of all can never be filled full. Moreover, Cerberus and the furies and yon privation of light [are idle tales, as well as all the rest, Ixion's wheel and black] Tartarus belching forth hideous fires from his throat: things which nowhere are nor, sooth to say, can be. But there is in life a dread of punish-ment for evil deeds, signal as the deeds are signal, and for atonement of guilt, the prison and the frightful hurling down from the rock, scourgings, executioners, the dungeon of the doomed, the pitch, the metal plate, torches; and even though these are wanting, yet the conscience-stricken mind through boding fears applies to itself goads and frightens itself with whips, and sees not meanwhile what end there can be of ills or what limit at last is to be set to punishments, and fears lest these very evils be enhanced after death. The life of fools at length becomes a hell here on earth.

This too you may sometimes say to yourself: "even worthy Ancus has quitted the light with his eyes, who was far, far better than thou, unconscionable man. And since then many other kings and caesars have been laid low, who lorded it over mighty nations. He too, even he who erst paved a way over the great sea and made a path for his legions to march over the deep and taught them to pass on foot over the salt pools and set at naught the roarings of the sea, trampling on them with his horses, had the light taken from him and shed forth his soul from his dying body. The son of the Scipios, thunderbolt of war, terror of Carthage, yielded his bones to earth just as if he were the lowest menial. Think too of the inventors of all sciences and graceful arts, think of the companions of the Heliconian maids; among whom Homer bore the sceptre without a peer, and he now sleeps the same sleep as others. Then there is Democritus, who, when a ripe old age had warned him that the memory-waking motions of his mind were waning, by his own spontaneous act offered up his head to death. Even Epicurus passed away, when his light of life had run its course, he who surpassed in intellect the race of man and quenched the light of all, as the ethereal sun arisen quenches the stars. Wilt thou then hesitate and think it a hardship to die? Thou for whom life is well nigh dead whilst yet thou livest and seest the light, who spendest the greater part of thy time in sleep and snorest wide awake and ceasest not to see visions and hast a mind troubled with groundless terror and canst not discover often what it is that ails thee, when, besotted man, thou art sore pressed on all sides with full many cares and goest astray tumbling about in the wayward wanderings of thy mind."

If, just as they are seen to feel that a load is on their mind which wears them out with its pressure, men might apprehend from what causes too it is produced and whence such a pile, if I may say so, of ill lies on their breast, they would not spend their life as we see them now for the most part do, not knowing, any one of them, what he means and wanting ever change of place as though he might lay his burden down. The man who is sick of home often issues forth from his large mansion, and as suddenly comes back to it, finding as he does that he is no better off abroad. He races to his country house, driving his jennets in headlong haste, as if hurrying to bring help to a house on fire; he yawns the moment he has reached the door of his house, or sinks heavily into sleep and seeks forgetfulness, or even in haste goes back again to town. In this way each man flies from himself (but self, from whom, as you may be sure is commonly the case, he cannot escape, clings to him in his own despite), hates too himself, because he is sick and knows not the cause of the malady; for if he could rightly see into this, relinquishing all else, each man would study to learn the nature of things, since the point at stake is the condition for eternity, not for one hour, in which mortals have to pass all the time which remains for them to expect after death.

Once more, what evil lust of life is this which constrains us with such force to be so mightily troubled in doubts and dangers? A sure term of life is fixed for mortals, and death cannot be shunned, but meet it we must. Moreover, we are ever engaged, ever involved in the same pursuits, and no new pleasure is struck out by living on; but whilst what we crave is wanting, it seems to transcend all the rest; then, when it has been gotten, we crave something else, and ever does the same thirst of life possess us, as we gape for it open-mouthed. Quite doubtful it is what fortune the future will carry with it or what chance will bring us or what end is at hand. Nor by prolonging life do we take one tittle from the time past in death nor can we fret anything away, whereby we may haply be a less long time in the condition of the dead. Therefore you may complete as many generations as you please during your life; none the less, however, will that everlasting death await you; and for no less long a time will he be no more in being, who beginning with today has ended his life, than the man who has died many months and years ago.

Book Four

I traverse the pathless haunts of the Pierides never yet
trodden by sole of man. I love to approach the untasted
springs and to quaff, I love to cull fresh flowers and gather for
my head a distinguished crown from spots whence the muses
have yet veiled the brows of none; first because I teach of
great things and essay to release the mind from the fast bonds
of religious scruples, and next because on a dark subject I pen
such lucid verses, o'erlaying all with the muses' charm. For
that too would seem to be not without good grounds: even
as physicians when they purpose to give nauseous wormwood
to children, first smear the rim round the bowl with the sweet
yellow juice of honey, that the unthinking age of children may
be fooled as far as the lips, and meanwhile drink up the bitter
draught of wormwood and though beguiled yet not be
betrayed, but rather by such means recover health and
strength: so I now, since this doctrine seems generally somewhat bitter to those by whom it has not been handled, and
the multitude shrinks back from it in dismay, have resolved
to set forth to you our doctrine in sweet-toned Pierian verse
and o'erlay it, as it were, with the pleasant honey of the
muses, if haply by such means I might engage your mind on
my verses, till such time as you apprehend all the nature of
things and throughly feel what use it has.

And now that I have taught what the nature of the mind is
and out of what things it is formed into one quickened being
with the body, and how it is dissevered and returns into its
first-beginnings, I will attempt to lay before you a truth
which most nearly concerns these questions, the existence of
things which we call idols of things: these, like films peeled
off from the surface of things, fly to and fro through the air,
and do likewise frighten our minds when they present them-

selves to us awake as well as in sleep, what time we behold strange shapes and idols of the light-bereaved, which have often startled us in appalling wise as we lay relaxed in sleep; this I will attempt, that we may not haply believe that souls break loose from Acheron or that shades fly about among the living or that any part of us is left behind after death, when the body and the nature of the mind destroyed together have taken their departure into their several first-beginnings.

I say then that pictures of things and thin shapes are emitted from things off their surface: these are like films or may each be named a rind, because each image bears an appearance and form like to the thing, whatever it is, from whose body it is shed and wanders forth. This you may learn, however dull of apprehension, from what follows. First of all, since among things open to sight many emit bodies, some in a state of loose diffusion, like smoke which logs of oak, heat which fires emit; some of a closer and denser texture, like the gossamer coats which at times cicadas doff in summer, and the films which calves at their birth cast from the surface of their body, as well as the vesture which the slippery serpent puts off among the thorns, for often we see the brambles enriched with their flying spoils: since these cases occur, a thin image likewise must be emitted from things off their surface. For why those films should drop off and withdraw from things rather than films which are really thin, not one tittle of proof can be given; especially since there are on the surface of things many minute bodies which may be discharged in the same order they had before and preserve the outline of the shape, and be discharged with far more velocity, inasmuch as they are less liable to get hampered, being few in number and stationed in the front rank. For without doubt we see many things discharge and freely give not only from the core and centre, as we said before, but from their surfaces, besides other things, colour itself. And this is commonly done by yellow and red and dark-blue awnings, when they are spread over large theatres and flutter and wave as they stretch across their poles and crossbeams; for then they dye the seated assemblage below and all the show of the stage and the richly attired company of the fathers, and compel them to dance about in their colour. And the more these objects are shut in all around by the walls of the theatre, the more do all of them within laugh on all hands, o'erlaid with graceful hues, the light of day being narrowed. Therefore since sheets of canvas emit colour from their surface, all things will naturally emit thin pictures too, since in each case alike they discharge from the surface. There are therefore as now shown sure outlines of shapes, which fly all about possessed of an exquisitely small thickness and cannot when separate be seen one at a time. Again, all smell, smoke, heat and other suchlike things stream off things in a state of diffusion, because while they are coming from the depths of the body, having arisen within it, they are torn in their winding passage, and there are no straight orifices to the paths, for them to make their way out by in a mass. But on the other hand, when a thin film of surface colour is discharged, there is nothing to rend it, since it is ready to hand stationed in front rank. Lastly, in the case of all idols which show themselves to us in mirrors, water or any other shining object, since their outsides are possessed of an appearance like to the things they represent, they must be formed of emitted images of things. There are therefore thin shapes and pictures like to the things which, though no one can see them one at a time, yet when thrown off by constant and repeated reflexion give back a visible image from the plane surface of mirrors; and in no other way, it would seem, can they be kept so entire that shapes are given back so exceedingly like each object.

Now mark, and learn how thin the nature of an image is. And first of all, since the first-beginnings are so far below the ken of our senses and much smaller than the things which our eyes begin to be unable to see, to strengthen yet more the proof of this also, learn in a few words how minutely fine are the beginnings of all things. First, living things are in some cases so very little that their third part cannot be seen at all. Of what size are we to suppose any gut of such creatures to be? Or the ball of the heart or the eyes? The limbs? Or any part of the frame? How small they must be! And then further, the several first-beginnings of which their soul and the nature of their mind must be formed—do you not perceive how fine, how minute they are? Again, in the case of all things which exhale from their body a pungent smell—allheal, nauseous wormwood, strong-scented southernwood and the bitter centauries—any one of which, if you happen to [feel it] lightly between two [fingers, will impregnate them with a strong smell] . . . but rather you are to know that idols of things wander about many in number in many ways, of no force, powerless to excite sense.

But lest haply you suppose that only those idols of things which go off from things and no others wander about, there are likewise those which are spontaneously begotten and are formed by themselves in this lower heaven which is called air: these, fashioned in many ways, are borne along on high and being in a fluid state, cease not to alter their appearance and change it into the outline of shapes of every possible kind; as we see clouds sometimes gather into masses on high and blot the calm, clear face of heaven, fanning the air with their motion. Thus often the faces of giants are seen to fly along and draw after them a far-spreading shadow; sometimes great mountains and rocks torn from the mountains are seen to go in advance and pass across the sun; and then some huge beast is observed to draw with it and bring on other storm clouds.

Now [I will proceed to show] with what ease and celerity they are begotten and how incessantly they flow and fall away from things. The outermost surface is ever streaming off from things and admits of being discharged: when this reaches some things, it passes through them, glass especially. But when it reaches rough stones or the matter of wood, it is then so torn that it cannot give back any idol. But when objects at once shining and dense have been put in its way, a mirror especially, none of these results has place: it can neither pass through it, like glass, nor can it be torn either; such perfect safety the polished surface minds to ensure. In consequence of this, idols stream back to us from such objects; and however suddenly at any moment you place anything opposite a mirror, an image shows itself: hence you may be sure that thin textures and thin shapes of things incessantly stream from their surface. Therefore many idols are begotten in a short time, so that the birth of such things is with good reason named a rapid one. And as the sun must send forth many rays of light in a short time in order that all things may be continually filled with it, so also for a like reason there must be carried away from things in a moment of time idols of things, many in number, in many ways, in all directions round; since to whatever part of them we present a mirror before their surfaces, other things correspond to these in the mirror of a like shape and like colour.

Moreover, though the state of heaven has just before been

of unsullied purity, with exceeding suddenness it becomes so hideously overcast that you might imagine all its darkness had abandoned Acheron throughout and filled up the great vaults of heaven: in such numbers, mid the frightful night of storm clouds that has gathered, do faces of black horror hang over us on high. Now there is no one who can tell how small a fraction of these an image is, or express that sum in language.

Now mark: how swift the motion is with which idols are borne along, and what velocity is assigned to them as they glide through the air, so that but a short hour is spent on a journey through long space, whatever the spot towards which they go with a movement of varied tendency, all this I will tell in sweetly worded rather than in many verses; as the short song of the swan is better than the loud noise of cranes scattered abroad amid the ethereal clouds of the south. First of all, we may very often observe that things which are light and made of minute bodies are swift. Of this kind are the light of the sun and its heat, because they are made of minute first things which are knocked forward, so to speak, and do not hesitate to pass through the space of air between, ever driven on by a blow following behind; for light on the instant is supplied by fresh light and brightness goaded to show its brightness in what you might call an ever on-moving team. Therefore in like manner idols must be able to scour in a moment of time through space unspeakable, first because they are exceeding small and there is a cause at their back to carry and impel them forward; next because when emitted they are possessed of so rare a texture that they can readily pass through any things and stream, as it were, through the space of air between. Again, if those minute bodies of things which are given out from the inmost depths of these things, as the light and heat of the sun, are seen in a moment of time to glide and spread themselves through the length and breadth of heaven, fly over sea and lands and flood the heaven, what then of those which stand ready posted in front rank, when they are discharged and nothing obstructs their egress, where, moreover, they are borne on with such winged rapidity? Do you not see how much faster and farther they must travel, scouring through many times the same amount of space in the time that the sunlight takes to spread over heaven? This too appears to be an eminently true proof of the velocity with which idols of things are borne along: as soon as ever the brightness of water is set down in the open air, if the heaven is starry, in a moment the clear, radiant constellations of ether imaged in the water correspond to those in the heaven. Now do you see in what a moment of time an image drops down from the borders of heaven to the borders of earth? Therefore again and again I repeat you must admit that bodies capable of striking the eyes and of provoking vision [constantly travel] with a marvellous [velocity]. Smells too incessantly stream from certain things; as does cold from rivers, heat from the sun, spray from the waves of the sea, that eater into walls near the shore. Various sounds also cease not to fly through the air. Then too a moist salt flavour often comes into the mouth, when we are moving about beside the sea; and when we look on at the mixing of a decoction of wormwood, its bitterness affects us. In such a constant stream from all these things the several qualities are carried and are transmitted in all directions round, and no delay, no respite in the flow is ever granted, since we constantly have feeling, and may at any time see, smell and hear anything.

Again, since a particular figure felt by the hands in the dark is known to be the same which is seen in the bright light of day, touch and sight must be excited by a quite similar cause. Well then, if we handle a square thing and it excites our attention in the dark, in the daylight what square thing will be able to fall on our sight, except the image of that thing? Therefore the cause of seeing, it is plain, lies in images and no thing can be perceived without them. Well, the idols of things I speak of are borne along all round and are discharged and transmitted in all directions; but because we can see with the eyes alone, the consequence is that, to whatever point we turn our sight, there all the several things meet and strike it with their shape and colour. And the image gives the power to see and the means to distinguish how far each thing is distant from us; for as soon as ever it is discharged, it pushes before it and impels all the air which lies between it and the eyes; and thus that air all streams through our eyes and brushes, so to say, the pupils and so passes through. The consequence is that we see how far distant each thing is. And the greater the quantity of air which is driven on before it and the larger the current which brushes our eyes, the more distant each different thing is seen to be. You must know these processes go on with extreme rapidity, so that at one and the same moment we see whatlike a thing is and how far distant it is. And this must by no means be deemed strange herein that, while the idols which strike the eyes cannot be seen one at a time, the things themselves are seen. For thus when the wind too beats us with successive strokes and when piercing cold streams, we are not wont to feel each single particle of that wind and cold, but rather the whole result; and then we perceive blows take effect on our body just as if something or other were beating it and giving us a sensation of its body outside. Again, when we thump a stone with a finger, we touch merely the outermost colour on the surface of the stone, and yet we do not feel that colour by our touch, but rather we feel the very hardness of the stone seated in its inmost depths.

Now mark, and learn why the image is seen beyond the mirror; for without doubt it is seen withdrawn far within. The case is just the same as with things which are viewed in their reality beyond a door, when it offers through it an unobstructed prospect and lets many things outside be seen from a house. That vision too is effected by two separate airs: first there is an air seen in such a case inside the doorway; next come the leaves of the door right and left; next a light outside brushes the eyes, then a second air, then those things outside which are viewed in their reality. Thus when the image of the mirror has first discharged itself, in coming to our sight it pushes forward and impels all the air which lies between it and the eyes, and enables us to see the whole of it before the mirror. But when we have perceived the mirror as well, at once the image which is conveyed from us reaches the mirror and then is reflected and comes back to our eyes, and drives on and rolls in front of it a second air and lets us see this before itself, and for this reason it looks so far withdrawn from the mirror. Wherefore again and again I repeat there is no cause at all to wonder why the images give back the reflexion from the surface of mirrors in the spot they do, since in both the given cases the result is produced by two airs. To proceed, the right side of our body is seen in mirrors to be on the left, because when the image comes and strikes on the plane of the mirror, it is not turned back unaltered, but is beaten out in a right line backwards, just as if you were to take a plaster mask before it is dry and dash it on a pillar or beam, and it forthwith were to preserve the lines of its features undistorted in front and were to strike out an exact copy of itself straight backwards. The result will be that the eye which was right will now be left; and conversely the left become the right. An image may also be so transmitted from one mirror to another that five or six idols are often produced. And thus all the things which lurk in the inmost corners of a house, however far they are withdrawn into tortuous recesses, may yet be all brought out through winding passages by the aid of a number of mirrors and be seen to be in the house. So unfailingly does the image reflect itself from mirror to mirror; and when the left side is presented, it becomes the right in the new image; then it is changed back again and turns round to what it was. Moreover, all mirrors which form little sides possessing a curvature resembling our side send back to us idols with their right corresponding to our right, either for this reason: because the image is transmitted from one mirror to another, and then after it has been twice struck out flies to us; or it may be because the image, when it has come to the mirror, wheels round, because the curved shape of the mirror teaches it to turn itself as we are turned. Again, you would think that idols step out and put down their foot at the same time with us and mimic our action, because from before whatever part of a mirror you move away, from that part forthwith no idols can be reflected; since nature constrains all things, when they are carried back and recoil from things, to be given back at angles equal to those at which they impinged.

Bright things, again, the eyes eschew and shun to look upon: the sun even blinds them, if you persist in turning them towards it, because its power is great and idols are borne through the clear air with great downward force from on high, and strike the eyes and disorder their fastenings. Moreover, any vivid brightness often burns the eyes, because it contains many seeds of fire which make a way in and beget pain in the eyes. Again, whatever the jaundiced look at becomes a green-ish-yellow, because many seeds of greenish-yellow stream from their body and meet the idols of things, and many too are mixed up in their eyes, and these by their infection tinge all things with sallow hues. Again, we see out of the dark things which are in the light for this reason: when the black air of darkness, being the nearer, has first entered and taken possession of the open eyes, the bright white air follows straightway after and cleanses them, so to say, and dispels the black shadows of the other air; for this is a great deal more nimble, a great deal more subtle and more efficacious. As soon as it has filled with light and opened up the passages of the eyes which the black air had before blocked up, forthwith the idols of things which are situated in the light follow and excite them so that we see. This we cannot do conversely in the dark out of the light, because the grosser air of darkness follows behind and quite fills all the openings and blocks up the passages of the eyes, not letting the idols of any things at all be thrown into the eyes to move them. Again, when we descry far off the square towers of a town, they often appear to be round for this reason: all the angles are seen from a distance to look obtuse, or rather are not seen at all, and their blow is lost and their stroke never makes its way to our sight, because while the idols are borne on through much air, the air by repeated collisions blunts the stroke perforce. When in this way all the angles have together eluded the sense, the stone structures are rounded off as if by the lathe; yet they do not look like the things which are close before us and really round, but somewhat resembling them as in shadowy outline. Our shadow likewise seems to move in the sunshine and to follow our steps and mimic our action; if you think forsooth that air deprived of life can step, imitating the motions and the actions of men; for that which we are wont to term shadow can be nothing but air devoid of light. Sure enough, because the earth in certain spots successively is deprived of light wherever we intercept it in moving about, while that part of it which we have quitted is filled with light, therefore that which was the shadow of our body seems to have always followed us unchanged in a direct line with us. For new rays of light ever pour in and the old are lost, just as if wool were drawn into the fire. Therefore the earth is readily stripped of light, and again filled, and cleanses itself from black shadows.

And yet in all this we do not admit that the eyes are cheated one whit. For it is their province to observe in what spot soever light and shade are; but whether the lights are still the same or not, and whether it is the same shadow which was in this spot that is now passing to that, or whether what we said a little before is not rather the fact, this the reason of the mind, and only it, has to determine; nor can the eyes know the nature of things. Do not then fasten upon the eyes this frailty of the mind. The ship in which we are sailing

moves on while seeming to stand still; that one which remains
at its moorings is believed to be passing by. The hills and
fields seem to be dropping astern, past which we are driving
our ship and flying under sail. The stars all seem to be at rest
fast fixed to the ethereal vaults, and yet are all in constant
motion, since they rise and then go back to their far-off
places of setting, after they have traversed the length of
heaven with their bright bodies. In like manner sun and moon
seem to stay in one place, bodies which simple fact proves
are carried on. And though between mountains rising up afar
off from amid the waters there opens out for fleets a free
passage of wide extent, yet a single island seems to be formed
out of them united into one. When children have stopped
turning round themselves, the halls appear to them to whirl
about and the pillars to course round to such a degree that
they can scarce believe that the whole roof is not threatening
to tumble down upon them. Again, when nature begins to
raise on high the sun's beam ruddy with bickering fires and
to lift it up above the mountains, those hills above which the
sun then seems to you to be, as blazing close at hand he dyes
them with his own fire, are distant from us scarce two thou-
sand arrow flights, yea, often scarce five hundred casts of a
javelin; and yet between them and the sun lie immense levels
of sea, spread out below the huge borders of ether, and many
thousands of lands are between, held by divers peoples and
races of wild beasts. Then a puddle of water not more than a
finger breadth deep, which stands between the stones in the
streets, offers a prospect beneath the earth of a reach as vast
as that with which the high yawning maw of heaven opens
out above the earth; so that you seem to discern clouds and
see the sky and all the other objects far withdrawn into that
wondrous sky beneath the earth. Again, when our stout horse
has stuck in the middle of a river and we have looked down
on the swift waters of the stream, some force seems to carry
athwart the current the body of the horse which is standing
still and to force it rapidly up the stream; and to whatever
point we cast our eyes about, all things seem to be carried on
and to be flowing in the same way as we are. Again, although
a portico runs in parallel lines from one end to the other and
stands supported by equal columns along its whole extent, yet
when from the top of it it is seen in its entire length, it
gradually forms the contracted top of a narrowing cone, until,

uniting roof with floor and all the right side with the left,
it has brought them together into the vanishing point of a
cone. To sailors on the sea the sun appears to rise out of the
waters and in the waters to set and bury his light; just because
they behold nothing but water and sky; that you may not
lightly suppose the credit of the senses to be shaken on all
hands. Then to people unacquainted with the sea, ships in
harbour seem to be all askew and, with poop fittings broken,
to be pressing up against the water. For whatever part of the
oars is raised above the salt water is straight, and the rudders
in their upper half are straight: the parts which are sunk
below the water level appear to be broken and bent round
and to slope up and turn back towards the surface and to be
so much twisted back as well nigh to float on the top of the
water. And when the winds carry the thinly scattered clouds
across heaven in the nighttime, then do the glittering signs
appear to glide athwart the rack and to be travelling on high
in a direction quite different to their real course. Then if our
hand chance to be placed beneath one eye and press it below,
through a certain sensation all things which we look at appear
then to become double as we look; the light of lamps brilliant
with flames to be double, double too the furniture through the
whole house, double men's faces and men's bodies. Again,
when sleep has chained down our limbs in sweet slumber and
the whole body is sunk in profound repose, yet then we seem
to ourselves to be awake and to be moving our limbs, and mid
the thick darkness of night we think we see the sun and the
daylight; and though in a confined room, we seem to be
passing to new climates, seas, rivers, mountains, and to be
crossing plains on foot and to hear noises, though the austere
silence of night prevails all round, and to be uttering speech
though quite silent. Many are the other things of this marvellous sort we see, which all seek to shake, as it were, the credit
of the senses: quite in vain, since the greatest part of these
cases cheats us on account of the mental suppositions which
we add of ourselves, taking those things as seen which have
not been seen by the senses. For nothing is harder than to
separate manifest facts from doubtful which straightway the
mind adds on of itself.

Again, if a man believe that nothing is known, he knows
not whether this even can be known, since he admits he
knows nothing. I will therefore decline to argue the case

against him who places himself with head where his feet should be. And yet granting that he knows this, I would still put this question, since he has never yet seen any truth in things, whence he knows what knowing and not knowing severally are, and what it is that has produced the knowledge of the true and the false and what has proved the doubtful to differ from the certain. You will find that from the senses first has proceeded the knowledge of the true and that the senses cannot be refuted. For that which is of itself to be able to refute things false by true things must from the nature of the case be proved to have the higher certainty. Well then, what must fairly be accounted of higher certainty than sense? Shall reason founded on false sense be able to contradict them, wholly founded as it is on the senses? And if they are not true, then all reason as well is rendered false. Or shall the ears be able to take the eyes to task, or the touch the ears? Again, shall the taste call in question this touch, or the nostrils refute or the eyes controvert it? Not so, I guess; for each apart has its own distinct office, each its own power; and therefore we must perceive what is soft and cold or hot by one distinct faculty, by another perceive the different colours of things and see all the qualities conjoined with colour. Taste too has its faculty apart; smells spring from one source, sounds from another. It must follow therefore than any one sense cannot confute any other. No, nor can any sense take itself to task, since equal credit must be assigned to it at all times. What therefore has at any time appeared true to each sense is true. And if reason shall be unable to explain away the cause why things which close at hand were square, at a distance looked round, it yet is better, if you are at a loss for the reason, to state erroneously the causes of each shape, than to let slip from your grasp on any side things manifest and ruin the groundwork of belief and wrench up all the foundations on which rest life and existence. For not only would all reason give way, life itself would at once fall to the ground, if you dare not trust the senses and shun precipices and all things else of this sort that are to be avoided, and pursue the opposite things. All that host of words then be sure is quite unmeaning, which has been drawn out in array against the senses. Once more, as in a building, if the rule first applied is wry, and the square is untrue and swerves from its straight lines, and if there is the slightest hitch in any part of the level, all the construction must be faulty, all must be wry, crooked, sloping, leaning forwards, leaning backwards, without symmetry, so that some parts seem ready to fall, others do fall, ruined all by the first erroneous measurements; so too all reason of things must needs prove to you distorted and false, which is founded on false senses.

And now to explain in what way the other senses do each perceive their several objects is the nowise arduous task which is still left.

In the first place, all sound and voice are heard when they have made their way into the ears and have struck with their body the sense of hearing. For voice too and sound you must admit to be bodily, since they are able to act upon the senses. Again, voice often abrades the throat, and shouting in passing forth makes the windpipe more rough: when, to whit, the first-beginnings of voices have risen up in larger mass and commenced to pass abroad through their strait passage, you are to know the door of the mouth, now crammed, itself is abraded. There is no doubt then that voices and words consist of bodily first-beginnings, with the power to hurt; nor can you fail to know how much of body is taken away and how much is withdrawn from men's very sinews and strength by a speech continued without interruption from the dawning brightness of morning to the shadow of black night, above all if it has been poured forth with much loud shouting. Voice therefore must be bodily, since a man by much speaking loses a portion from his body. Next roughness of voice comes from roughness of the first-beginnings, as smoothness is produced from smoothness. Nor are the first-beginnings of like shape which pierce the ears in these two cases: when the trumpet brays dully in deep, low tones, the barbarian country roused echoing back the hoarse, hollow sound, and when swans from the headstrong torrents of Helicon raise their clear-toned dirge with plaintive voice.

When therefore we force these voices forth from the depths of our body and discharge them straight out at the mouth, the pliant tongue, deft fashioner of words, gives them articulate utterance and the structure of the lips does its part in shaping them. Therefore when the distance is not long between the point from which each several voice has started and that at which it arrives, the very words too must be plainly heard and distinguished syllable by syllable; for each voice retains its structure and retains its shape. But if the space between be more than is suitable, the words must be huddled together in passing through much air and the voice be disorganised in its flight through the same. Therefore it is that you can hear a sound, yet cannot distinguish what the meaning of the words is: so huddled and hampered is the voice when it comes. Again, a single word often stirs the ears of a whole assembly of people, when uttered by the crier's mouth. One voice therefore in a moment starts asunder into many voices, since it distributes itself separately into all the ears, stamping upon them the form and distinct sound of the word. But such of the voices as do not fall directly on the ears are carried past and lost, fruitlessly dispersed in air; some, striking upon solid spots, are thrown back and give back a sound and sometimes mock by an echo of the word. When you fully perceive all this, you may explain to yourself and others how it is that in lonely spots rocks give back in regular succession forms of words like to those sent forth, as we seek our comrades straying about among the darkened hills and with loud voice call upon them scattered abroad. I have seen places give back as many as six or seven voices, when you sent forth one: in such wise did the very hills dash back on hills and repeat the words thus trained to come back. These spots the people round fancy that the goat-footed satyrs and nymphs inhabit, and tell that they are the fauns by whose night-pervading noise and sportive play, as they declare, the still silence is broken and sounds produced of stringed instruments and sweet plaintive melodies, such as the pipe pours forth when beaten by the fingers of the players; the country people hearing far and wide, what time Pan, nodding the piny covering of his head half a beast's, oft runs over the gaping reeds with curved lip, making the pipe without ceasing to pour forth its woodland song. Other suchlike prodigies and marvels they tell of, that they may not haply be thought to inhabit lonely places, abandoned even by the gods. On this account they vaunt such wonders in their stories or are led on by some other reason; inasmuch as the whole race of man is all too greedy after listening ears.

To proceed, you need not wonder how it is that through places through which the eyes cannot see plain things, voices come and strike the ears. We often see a conversation go on even through closed doors, sure enough because the voice can pass uninjured through the winding openings of things, while idols refuse to pass: they are torn to shreds, if the openings through which they glide are not straight, like those of glass, through which every image passes. Again, a voice distributes itself in all directions, since voices are begotten one out of another, when a single voice has once gone forth and sprung into many, as a spark of fire is often wont to distribute itself into its constituent fires. Therefore places are filled with voices, which though far withdrawn out of view yet are all in commotion and stirred by sound. But idols all proceed in straight courses as soon as they have been discharged; and therefore you can never see beyond a wall, but you may hear voices outside it. And yet this very voice even in passing through the walls of houses is blunted and enters the ears in a huddled state, and we seem to hear the sound rather than the actual words.

The tongue and palate, whereby we perceive flavour, have not in them anything that calls for longer explanation or offers more difficulty. In the first place, we perceive flavour in the mouth when we press it out in chewing our food, in the same way as when one haply begins to squeeze with his hand and dry a sponge full of water. Next, the whole of what we press out distributes itself through the cavities of the palate and the intricate openings of the porous tongue. Therefore when the bodies of oozing flavour are smooth, they pleasantly touch and pleasantly feel all the parts about the moist, exuding quarters of the palate. But on the other hand, when they rise in a mass they puncture and tear the sense according to the degree in which they are pervaded by roughness. Next, the pleasure from the flavour reaches as far as the palate; when, however, it has passed down through the throat, there is no pleasure while it is all distributing itself into the frame. And it makes no matter what the food is with which the body is nurtured, provided you can digest what you take and transmit it into the frame and keep the stomach in an equable condition of moistness.

I will now explain how it is that different food is pleasant and nutritious for different creatures; also why that which to some is nauseous and bitter may yet to others seem passing sweet; and why in these matters the difference and discrepancy is so great that what to one man is food, to another is rank poison: thus there may exist a serpent which on being touched by a man's spittle wastes away and destroys itself by gnawing its body. Again, hellebore for us is rank poison, but helps to fatten goats and quails. That you may know how this comes to pass, first of all you must remember what we have said before, that the seeds which are contained in things are mixed up in manifold ways. Again, all living creatures soever which take food, even as they are unlike on the outside, and, differing in each after its kind, an exterior contour of limbs bounds them, so likewise are they formed of seeds of varying shape. Again, since the seeds differ, there must be a discrepancy in the spaces between and the passages, which we name openings, in all the limbs and mouth and palate as well. Some seeds therefore must be smaller, some larger; some things must have three-cornered, others square seeds; many seeds must be round, some many-angled after many fashions. For as the relation between the shapes of seeds and their motions require, the openings also must differ accordingly in their shapes; and the passages must vary, as varies the texture formed by the seeds which bound them. For this reason, when that which is sweet to some becomes bitter to others, for that creature to whom it is sweet the smoothest bodies must enter the cavities of the palate with power to feel them all over; but on the other hand, in the case of those to whom the same thing is bitter within, rough and barbed seeds sure enough pass down the throat. It is easy now from these principles to understand all particular cases: thus when a fever has attacked anyone from too great a flow of bile, or a violent disease has been excited in any other way, thereupon the whole body is disordered and all the arrangements of particles then and there changed; the consequence of which is that the bodies which before were suited to excite sensation, suit no more; and those fit it better which are able to make their way in and beget a bitter sense. Both kinds, for instance, are mixed up in the flavour of honey: a point we have often proved before.

Now mark me, and I will discuss the way in which the contact of smell affects the nostrils: and first there must be many things from which a varied flow of smells streams and rolls on; and we must suppose that they thus stream and discharge and disperse themselves among all things alike; but one smell fits itself better to one creature, another to another on account of their unlike shapes; and therefore bees are drawn on by the smell of honey through the air to a very great distance, and so are vultures by carcases. Also the far-reaching power of scent in dogs leads them on whithersoever the cloven hoof of wild beasts has carried them in their course; and the smell of man is felt far away by the savior of the Romans' citadel, the bright white goose. Thus different scents assigned to different creatures lead each to its appropriate food and constrain them to recoil from nauseous poison, and in this way the races of beasts are preserved.

Of all these different smells then which strike the nostrils, one may reach to a much greater distance than another; though none of them is carried so far as sound, as voice, to say nothing of things which strike the eyesight and provoke vision. For in its mazy course each comes slowly on and is sooner lost, being gradually dispersed into the readily receiving expanse of air; first because, coming out of its depths, it with difficulty discharges itself from the thing: for the fact that all things are found to have a stronger smell when crushed, when pounded, when broken up by fire, shows that odours stream and withdraw from the inner parts of things; next you may see that smell is formed of larger first-beginnings than voice, since it does not pass through stone walls, through which voice and sound are borne without fail. For this reason also you will find that it is not so easy to trace out in what quarter a thing which smells is situated; for the blow cools down as it loiters through the air, and the courier particles of things are no longer hot when they finish their race to sense; for which reason dogs are often at fault and lose the scent.

But what I have said is not found in smells and in the class of flavours only, but also the forms and colours of things are not all so well suited to the senses of all, but that some will be more distressing to the sight than others. Moreover, ravenous lions cannot face and bear to gaze upon a cock with flapping wings putting night to rout and wont to summon morning with shrill voice: in such wise they at once bethink themselves of flight, because sure enough in the body of cocks are certain seeds, and these, when they have been discharged into the eyes of lions, bore into the pupils and cause such sharp pain that fierce though they be, they cannot continue to face them; while at the same time these things cannot hurt at all our sight, either because they do not enter in or because the moment they enter, a free passage out of the eyes is granted them, so that they cannot by staying behind hurt the eyes in any part.

Now mark, and hear what things move the mind, and learn in a few words whence the things which come into it do come. I say first of all that idols of things wander about many in number in many ways in all directions round, extremely thin; and these, when they meet, readily unite, like a cobweb or piece of gold leaf. For these idols are far thinner in texture than those which take possession of the eyes and provoke vision, since these enter in through the porous parts of the body and stir the fine nature of the mind within and provoke sensation. Therefore we see centaurs and limbs of Scylla and Cerberus-like faces of dogs and idols of those who are dead and whose bones earth holds in its embrace; since idols of every kind are everywhere borne about, partly those which are spontaneously produced within the air, partly all those which withdraw from various things and those which are formed by compounding the shapes of these. For assuredly no image of centaur is formed out of a live one, since no such nature of living creature ever existed; but when images of a horse and a man have by chance come together, they readily adhere at once, as we said before, on account of their fine nature and thin texture. All other things of the kind are produced in like fashion. And when these from extreme lightness are borne on with velocity, as I showed before, any one subtle composite image you like readily moves the mind by a single stroke; for the mind is fine and is itself wondrously nimble.

That all this is done as I relate, you may easily learn from what follows. So far as the one result is like the other, that which we see with the mind and with the eyes must be produced in the like way. Well then, since I have shown that I perceive, for instance, a lion by means of idols which provoke the eyes, you may be sure that the mind is moved in a like way, which by means of idols sees a lion or anything else just as well as the eyes, with this difference, that it perceives much thinner idols. And when sleep has prostrated the body, for no other reason does the mind's intelligence wake, except because the very same idols provoke our minds which provoke them when we are awake, and to such a degree that we seem without a doubt to perceive him whom life has left and death and earth gotten hold of. This nature constrains to come to pass because all the senses of the body are then hampered and at rest throughout the limbs and cannot refute the unreal by real things. Moreover, memory is prostrate and relaxed in sleep and protests not that he has long been in the grasp of death and destruction whom the mind believes it sees alive. Furthermore, it is not strange that idols move and throw about their arms and other limbs in regular measure; for sometimes in sleep an image is seen to do this: when the first, to wit, has gone and a second then been born in another posture, that former one seems to have altered its attitude. This, remember, you must assume to take place with exceeding celerity: so great is the velocity, so great the store of things; so great in any one unit of time that sense can seize is the store of particles, out of which the supply may go on.

And here many questions present themselves and many points must be cleared up by us, if we desire to give a plain exposition of things. The first question is why, when the wish has occurred to anyone to think of a thing, his mind on the instant thinks of that very thing. Do idols observe our will, and so soon as we will does an image present itself to us, if sea, if earth, ay or heaven, is what we wish? Assemblies of men, a procession, feasts, battles, everything in short does nature at command produce and provide? And though to increase the marvel, the mind of others in the same spot and room is thinking of things all quite different. What again are we to say, when we see in sleep idols advance in measured tread and move their pliant limbs, pliant I say, when in nimble wise they put out each arm in turn and represent to the eyes over and over again an action with foot that moves in time? Idols, to wit, are imbued with art and move about well-trained, to be able in the nighttime to exhibit such plays. Or will this rather be the truth: because in one unit of time, when we can perceive it by sense and while one single word is uttered, many latent times are contained which reason finds to exist, therefore in any time you please all the several idols are at hand ready prepared in each several place. And because they are so thin, the mind can see distinctly only those which it strains itself to see; therefore all that there are besides are lost, save only such as it has taken to itself. Moreover, it makes itself ready and hopes to see that which follows upon each thing; therefore the result does follow. Do you not see that the eyes also, when they essay to discern things which are thin and fine, strain themselves and make themselves ready, and without that we cannot see distinctly? And yet you may observe even in things which are plain before us, that if you do not attend, it is just as if the thing were all the time away and far distant. What wonder then, if the mind loses all other things save those with which it is itself earnestly occupied? Then too from small indications we draw the widest inferences and by our own fault entangle ourselves in the meshes of self-delusion.

Sometimes it happens too that an image of the same kind is not supplied, but what before was a woman, turns out in our hands to have changed into a man; or a different face and age succeeds to the first. But sleep and forgetfulness prevent us from feeling surprise at this.

And herein you should desire with all your might to shun the weakness, with a lively apprehension to avoid the mistake of supposing that the bright lights of the eyes were made in order that we might see; and that the tapering ends of the shanks and hams are attached to the feet as a base in order to enable us to step out with long strides; or again that the fore-arms were slung to the stout upper arms and ministering hands given us on each side, that we might be able to discharge the needful duties of life. Other explanations of like sort which men give, one and all put effect for cause through wrongheaded reasoning; since nothing was born in the body that we might use it, but that which is born begets for itself a use: thus seeing did not exist before the eyes were born, nor the employment of speech ere the tongue was made; but rather the birth of the tongue was long anterior to language and the ears were made long before sound was heard, and all the limbs, I trow, existed before there was any employment for them: they could not therefore have grown for the purpose of being used. But on the other hand, engaging in the strife of battle and mangling the body and staining the limbs with gore were in vogue long before glittering darts ever flew; and nature prompted to shun a wound or ever the left arm by the help of art held up before the person the defence of a shield. Yes and consigning the tired body to rest is much older than a soft-cushioned bed, and the slaking of thirst had birth before cups. These things therefore which have been invented in accordance with the uses and wants of life may well be believed to have been discovered for the purpose of being used. Far otherwise is it with all those things which first were born, then afterwards made known the purposes to which they might be put; at the head of which class we see the senses and the limbs. Wherefore again and again I repeat, it is quite impossible to believe that they could have been made for the duties which they discharge.

It ought likewise to cause no wonder that the nature of the body of each living creature absolutely requires food. I have shown that bodies ebb away and withdraw from things, many in number in many ways; but most numerous must be those which withdraw from living things; for because these are tried by active motion, and many particles are pressed out from the depths of the frame and carried off by sweating, many breathed out through the mouth, when they pant from exhaustion, from such causes the body becomes rarefied and the whole nature undermined; and this state is attended by pain. Food therefore is taken in order to give support to the frame and recruit the strength by its infusion, and to close up the open-mouthed craving for meat throughout limbs and veins. The moisture too passes into all the parts which call for moisture; and many accumulated bodies of heat which cause a burning in our stomach, the approach of liquid scatters and quenches as if they were fire, so that dry heat can no longer parch the frame. In this way then, you see, gasping thirst is drenched out of our body, in this way the hungry craving is satisfied.

Now how it comes to pass that we are able to step out when we please, and how it is given us to move about our limbs, and what cause is wont to push forward the great load of this our body I will tell: do you take in my words. I say that idols of walking first present themselves to our mind and strike on the mind, as we said before; then the will arises: for no one begins to do anything until his mind has first determined what it wills. From the very fact that it first determines such thing, there is an image of that thing. When therefore the mind bestirs itself in such a way as to will to walk and step out, it strikes at the same moment the force of the soul which is spread over the whole body throughout the limbs and frame; and this is easily done, since the whole is held in close union with the mind. Next the soul in its turn strikes the body, and thus the whole mass by degrees is pushed on and set in motion. Then again the body becomes also rarefied, and the air, as you see its nature is, being always so nimble in moving, comes and passes in great quantity through the opened pores and is thus distributed into the most minute parts of the body. In this way then, by these two causes acting in two different ways, the body after the fashion of ships is carried on by sails and wind. And herein it need not excite any surprise that such very minute bodies can steer so great a body and turn about the whole of this our load; for wind, though fine, with subtle body drives and pushes on a large ship of large moving mass and one hand directs it, however great the speed at which it is going, and one rudder steers it to any point you like; and by means of blocks of pulleys and treadwheels a machine stirs many things, though of great weight, and raises them up with slight effort.

Now by what means yon sleep lets a stream of repose over the limbs and dispels from the breast the cares of the mind, I will tell in sweetly worded rather than in many verses; as the short song of the swan is better than the loud noise of cranes scattered abroad amid the ethereal clouds of the south. Do you lend me a nice ear and a keen mind, that you may not deny what I say to be possible and secede with breast disdainfully rejecting the words of truth, you yourself being in fault the while and unable to discern. Sleep mainly takes place when the force of the soul has been scattered about through the frame, and in part has been forced abroad and taken its departure, and in part has been thrust back and has withdrawn into the depths of the body; after that the limbs are relaxed and droop. For there is no doubt that this sense exists in us by the agency of the soul; and when sleep obstructs the action of this sense, then we must assume that our soul has been disordered and forced abroad; not indeed all; for then the body would lie steeped in the everlasting chill of death. Where no part of the soul remained behind concealed in the limbs, as fire remains concealed when buried under much ash, whence could sense be suddenly rekindled through the limbs, as flame can spring up from hidden fire?

But by what means this change of condition is accomplished and from what the soul can be disordered and the body grow faint, I will explain: do you mind that I waste not my words on the wind. In the first place, the body in its outer side, since it is next to and is touched by the air, must be thumped and beaten by its repeated blows; and for this reason all things as a rule are covered either by a hide or else by shells or by a callous skin or by bark. When creatures breathe, this air at the same time buffets the inner side also, as it is inhaled and exhaled. Therefore since the body is beaten on both sides alike and blows arrive by means of the small apertures at the primal parts and primal elements of our body, there gradually ensues a sort of breaking up throughout our limbs, the arrangements of the first-beginnings of body and mind getting disordered. Then next a part of the soul is forced out and a part withdraws into the inner recesses; a part too scattered about through the frame cannot get united together and so act and be acted upon by motion; for nature intercepts all communication and blocks up all the passages; and therefore sense retires deep into the frame as the motions are all altered. And since there is nothing, as it were, to lend support to the frame, the body becomes weak and all the limbs are faint, the arms and eyelids droop and the hams even in bed often give way under you and relax their powers. Then sleep follows on food, because food produces just the same effects as air, while it is distributed into all the veins; and that sleep is much the heaviest which you take when full or tired, because then the greatest number of bodies fall into disorder, bruised by much exertion. On the same principle the soul comes in part to be forced more deeply into the frame, and there is also a more copious emission of it abroad, and at the same time it is more divided and scattered in itself within you.

And generally to whatever pursuit a man is closely tied down and strongly attached, on whatever subject we have previously much dwelt, the mind having been put to a more than usual strain in it, in sleep we for the most part fancy that we are engaged in the same; lawyers think they plead causes and draw up covenants of sale, generals that they fight and engage in battle, sailors that they wage and carry on war with the winds, we think we pursue our task and investigate the nature of things constantly and consign it when discovered to writings in our native tongue. So all other pursuits and arts are seen for the most part during sleep to occupy and mock the minds of men. And whenever men have given during many days in succession undivided attention to games, we generally see that after they have ceased to perceive these with their senses, there yet remain passages open in the mind through which the same idols of things may enter. Thus for many days those same objects present themselves to the eyes, so that even when awake they see dancers as they think moving their pliant limbs, and receive into the ears the clear music of the harp and speaking strings, and behold the same spectators and at the same time the varied decorations of the stage in all their brilliancy. So great is the influence of zeal and inclination, so great is the influence of the things in which men have been habitually engaged, and not men only but all living creatures. Thus you will see stout horses, even when their bodies are lying down, yet in their sleep sweat and pant without ceasing and strain their powers to the utmost as if for the prize, or as if the barriers were thrown open . . . And often during soft repose the dogs of hunters do yet all at once throw about their legs and suddenly utter cries and repeatedly snuff the air with their nostrils, as though they had found and were on the tracks of wild beasts; and after they are awake often chase the shadowy idols of stags, as though they saw them in full flight, until they have shaken off their delusions and come to themselves again. And the fawning brood of dogs brought up tame in the house haste to shake their body and raise it up from the ground, as if they beheld unknown faces and features. And the fiercer the different breeds are, the greater rage they must display in sleep. But the various kinds of birds flee and suddenly in the nighttime trouble with their wings the groves of the gods, when in gentle sleep hawks have appeared to fly in pursuit and to show fight and offer battle. Again, the minds of men which pursue great aims under great emotions often during sleep pursue and carry on the same in like manner; kings take by storm, are taken, join battle, raise a loud cry as if stabbed on the spot. Many struggle hard and utter groans in pain, and as if gnawed by the bite of panther or cruel lion, fill all the place with loud cries. Many during sleep speak of important affairs and have often and often disclosed their own guilt. Many meet death; many, as if tumbling down from high precipices to the ground with their whole body, are scared with terror and after sleep, as if they were out of their judgment, scarce come to themselves again, quite disordered by their body's turmoil. Again, a thirsty man sits down beside a river or a pleasant spring and gulps down well nigh all the stream. Cleanly people often, when sound asleep, believing that they are lifting their dress beside a urinal or the public vessels, pour forth the filtered liquid of their whole body, and the Babylonian coverlets of surpassing brilliancy are drenched. Then too those into the boiling currents of whose age seed is for the first time passing, when the ripe fulness of days has produced it in their limbs, encounter idols from without from what body soever, harbingers of a glorious face and a beautiful bloom, which stir and excite the appropriate portions of the frame and often occasion fruitless anticipations of the pleasures of love.

That seed we have spoken of before is stirred up in us, as soon as ripe age fortifies the frame. For as different causes set in motion and excite different things, so from man the sole influence of man draws forth human seed. As soon then as it has been forced out from and quits its proper seats, throughout the limbs and frame it withdraws itself from the whole body and meets together in appropriate places and rouses forthwith the appropriate parts of the body. The places are excited and swell with seed, and the inclination arises to emit that seed towards that to which the fell desire all tends, and the body seeks that object from which the mind is wounded by love; for all as a rule fall towards their wound and the blood spirts out in that direction whence comes the stroke by which we are struck; and if he is at close quarters, the red stream covers the foe. Thus then he who gets a hurt from the weapons of Venus, whatever be the object that hits him, be it a woman breathing love from her whole body, he inclines to the quarter whence he is wounded and yearns to unite with it and join body with body; for a mute desire gives a presage of the pleasure.

This pleasure is for us Venus; from that desire is the Latin name of love, from that desire has first trickled into the heart yon drop of Venus' honeyed joy, succeeded soon by chilly care; for though that which you yearn for is away, yet idols of it are at hand and its sweet name is present to the ears. But it is meet to fly idols and scare away all that feeds love and turn your mind on another object, distract your passion elsewhere and not keep it, with your thoughts once set on one object by love of it, and so lay up for yourself care and unfailing pain. For the sore gathers strength and becomes inveterate by feeding, and every day the madness grows in violence and the misery becomes aggravated, unless you erase the first wounds by new blows and first heal them when yet fresh, roaming abroad after Venus the pandemian, or transfer to something else the emotions of your mind.

Nor is he who shuns love without the fruits of Venus, but rather enjoys those blessings which are without any pain: doubtless the pleasure from such things is more unalloyed for the healthy-minded than for the lovesick; for in the very moment of enjoying, the burning desire of lovers wavers and wanders undecided, and they cannot tell what first to enjoy with eyes and hands. What they have sought, they tightly squeeze and cause pain of body and often imprint their teeth on the lips and clash mouth to mouth in kissing, because the pleasure is not pure and there are hidden strings which stimulate to hurt even that whatever it is from which spring those germs of frenzy. But Venus with light hand breaks the force of these pains during love, and the fond pleasure mingled therein reins in the bites. For in this there is hope, that from the same body whence springs their burning desire, their flame may likewise be quenched; the direct contrary of which nature protests to be the case; and this is the one thing of all in which, when we have most of it, then all the more the breast burns with fell desire. Meat and drink are taken into the body; and as they can fill up certain fixed parts, in this way the craving for drink and bread is easily satisfied; but from the face and beautiful bloom of man nothing is given into the body to enjoy save flimsy idols; a sorry hope which is often snatched off by the wind. As when in sleep a thirsty man seeks to drink and water is not given to quench the burning in his frame, but he seeks the idols of waters and toils in vain and thirsts as he drinks in the midst of the torrent stream, thus in love Venus mocks lovers with idols, nor can bodies satisfy them by all their gazing upon them nor can they with their hands rub aught off the soft limbs, wandering undecided over the whole body. At last when they have united and enjoy the flower of age, when the body now has a presage of joys and Venus is in the mood to sow the fields of woman, they greedily clasp each other's body and suck each other's lips and breathe in, pressing meanwhile teeth on each other's mouth; all in vain, since they can rub nothing off nor enter and pass each with his whole body into the other's body; for so sometimes they seem to will and strive to do: so greedily are they held in the chains of Venus, while their limbs melt, overpowered by the might of the pleasure. At length when the gathered desire has gone forth, there ensues for a brief while a short pause in the burning passion; and then returns the same frenzy, then comes back the old madness, when they are at a loss to know what they really desire to get, and cannot find what device is to conquer that mischief; in such utter uncertainty they pine away by a hidden wound.

Then too they waste their strength and ruin themselves by the labour, then too their life is passed at the beck of another. Meanwhile their estate runs away and is turned into Babylonian coverlets; duties are neglected and their good name staggers and sickens. On her feet laugh elastic and beautiful Sicyonian shoes, yes, and large emeralds with green light are set in gold and the sea-coloured dress is worn constantly and, much used, drinks in the sweat. The noble earnings of their fathers are turned into hairbands, headdresses; sometimes are changed into a sweeping robe and Alideusian and Cean dresses. Feasts set out with rich coverlets and viands, games, numerous cups, perfumes, crowns, garlands are prepared; all in vain, since out of the very wellspring of delights rises up something of bitter, to pain amid the very flowers; either when the conscience-stricken mind haply gnaws itself with remorse to think that it is passing a life of sloth and ruining itself in brothels, or because she has launched forth some word and left its meaning in doubt and it cleaves to the lovesick heart and burns like living fire, or because it fancies she casts her eyes too freely about or looks on another, and it sees in her face traces of a smile.

And these evils are found in love that is lasting and highly prosperous; but in crossed and hopeless love are ills such as you may seize with closed eyes, past numbering; so that it is better to watch beforehand in the manner I have prescribed, and be on your guard not to be drawn in. For to avoid falling into the toils of love is not so hard as, after you are caught, to get out of the nets you are in and to break through the strong meshes of Venus. And yet even when you are entangled and held fast you may escape the mischief, unless you stand in your own way and begin by overlooking all the defects of her mind or those of her body, whoever it is whom you court and woo. For this men usually do, blinded by passion, and attribute to the beloved those advantages which are not really theirs. We therefore see women in ways manifold deformed and ugly to be objects of endearment and held in the highest admiration. And one lover jeers at others and advises them to propitiate Venus, since they are troubled by a disgraceful passion, and often, poor wretches, give no thought to their own ills, greatest of all. The black is a brune, the filthy and rank has not the love of order; the cat-eyed is a miniature Pallas, the stringy and wizened a gazelle; the dumpy and dwarfish is one of the graces, from top to toe undiluted esprit; the big and overgrown is awe-inspiring and full of dignity. She is tongue-tied, cannot speak, then she has a lisp; the dumb is bashful; then the fire-spit, the teasing, the gossiping turns to a shining lamp. One becomes a slim darling then when she cannot live from want of flesh; and she is only spare, who is half-dead with cough. Then the fat and big-breasted is a Ceres' self, big-breasted from Iacchus; the pug-nosed is a she-Silenus and a satyress; the thick-lipped a very kiss. It were tedious to attempt to report other things of the kind. Let her, however, be of ever so great dignity of appearance, such that the power of Venus goes forth from all her limbs; yet there are others too; yet have we lived without her before; yet does she do, and we know that she does, in all things the same as the ugly woman; and fumigates herself, poor wretch, with nauseous perfumes, her very maids running from her and giggling behind her back. But the lover, when shut out, often in tears covers the threshold with flowers and wreaths and anoints the haughty doorposts with oil of marjoram and imprints kisses, poor wretch, on the doors. When, however, he has been admitted, if on his approach but one single breath should come in his way, he would seek specious reasons for departing, and the long-conned, deep-drawn complaint would fall to the ground; and then he would blame his folly, on seeing that he had attributed to her more than it is right to concede to a mortal. Nor is this unknown to our Venuses; wherefore all the more they themselves hide with the utmost pains all that goes on behind the scenes of life from those whom they wish to retain in the chains of love; but in vain, since you may yet draw forth from her mind into the light all these things and search into all her smiles; and if she is of a fair mind and not troublesome, overlook them in your turn and make allowance for human failings.

Nor does the woman sigh always with feigned passion, when she locks in her embrace and joins with her body the man's body and holds it, sucking his lips into her lips and drinking in his kisses. Often she does it from the heart, and seeking mutual joys courts him to run the complete race of love. And in no other way could birds, cattle, wild beasts, sheep and mares submit to bear the males, except because the very exuberance of nature in the females is in heat and burns and joyously draws in the Venus of the covering males. See you not too how those whom mutual pleasure has chained are often tortured in their common chains? How often in the highways do dogs, desiring to separate, eagerly pull different ways with all their might, while all the time they are held fast in the strong fetters of Venus! This they would never do, unless they experienced mutual joys, strong enough to force them into the snare and hold them in its meshes. Wherefore again and again I repeat, there is a common pleasure.

And when haply in mixing her seed with the man's the woman by sudden force has overpowered and seized for herself his force, then children are formed from the mothers' seed like to the mothers, as from the fathers' seed like to the fathers. But those whom you see with a share of both forms, blending equally the features of the parents, grow from the union of the father's body and the mother's blood, when the mutual ardour of desire working in concert has brought and clashed together the seeds roused throughout the frame by the goads of Venus; and neither of the two has gotten the mastery nor has been mastered. Sometimes too the children may spring up like their grandfathers and often resemble the forms of their grandfathers' fathers, because the parents often keep concealed in their bodies many first-beginnings mixed in many ways, which first proceeding from the original stock one father hands down to the next father; and then from these Venus produces forms after a manifold chance and repeats not only the features, but the voices and hair of their forefathers. And the female sex equally springs from the father's seed and males go forth equally formed from the mother's body; since these distinctions no more proceed from the fixed seed of one or other parent than our faces and bodies and limbs: the birth is always formed out of the two seeds; and whichever parent that which is produced more resembles, of that parent it has more than an equal share; as you may equally observe, whether it is a male child or a female birth.

Nor do the divine powers debar anybody from the power of

begetting, forbidding him ever to receive the name of father from sweet children and forcing him to pass his life in a barren wedlock; as men commonly fancy when in sorrow they drench the altars with much blood and pile the raised altars with offerings, to make their wives pregnant with abundant seed. In vain they weary the divinity of the gods and the sacred lots. They are barren sometimes from the too great thickness of the seed, sometimes from its undue fluidity and thinness: because the thin is unable to get a firm hold on the right spots, it at once passes away and is repelled and withdrawn abortively; since by others again a too thick seed is discharged in a state more solid than is suitable, it either does not fly forth with so prolonged a stroke or cannot equally pass into the proper spots or when it has passed in with difficulty mixes with the woman's seed. For well-assorted matches are found to be of great importance; and some males impregnate some females more readily than others, and other females conceive and become pregnant more readily from other males. And many women have hitherto been barren during several marriages and have yet in the end found mates from whom they could conceive children and be enriched with a sweet offspring. And often even for those, to whom hitherto wives, however fruitful, had been unable in their house to bear, has been found a compatible nature, enabling them to fortify their age with sons. Of such great importance is it, in order that seeds may agree and blend with seeds in a way to promote birth, whether the thick comes into contact with the fluid and the fluid with the thick. And on this point it matters much on what diet life is supported; for by some foods seed is thickened in the limbs, and by others again is thinned and wasted. And in what modes the intercourse goes on is likewise of very great moment; for women are commonly thought to conceive more readily after the manner of wild beasts and quadrupeds, because the seeds in this way can find the proper spots in consequence of the position of the body. Nor have wives the least use for effeminate motions: a woman hinders and stands in the way of her own conceiving, when thus she acts; for she drives the furrow out of the direct course and path of the share and turns away from the proper spots the stroke of the seed. And thus for their own ends harlots are wont to move, in order not to conceive and lie in childbed frequently, and at the same time to render Venus more attractive to men. This our wives would seem to have no need for.

Sometimes too by no divine grace and arrows of Venus a sorry woman of inferior beauty comes to be loved; for the woman sometimes by her own acts and accommodating manners and by elegant neatness of person readily habituates you to pass your life with her. Moreover, custom renders love attractive; for that which is struck by oft-repeated blows, however lightly, yet after long course of time is overpowered and gives way. See you not too that drops of water falling on rocks after long course of time scoop a hole through these rocks?

Book Five

WHO is able with powerful genius to frame a poem worthy
of the grandeur of the things and these discoveries, or who
is so great a master of words as to be able to devise praises
equal to the deserts of him who left to us such prizes won and
earned by his own genius? None, methinks, who is formed of
mortal body. For if we must speak as the acknowledged
grandeur of the things itself demands, a god he was, a god,
most noble Memmius, who first found out that plan of life
which is now termed wisdom, and who by trained skill res-
cued life from such great billows and such thick darkness
and moored it in so perfect a calm and in so brilliant a light.
Compare the godlike discoveries of others in old times: Ceres
is famed to have pointed out to mortals corn, and Liber the
vine-born juice of the grape; though life might well have
subsisted without these things, as we are told some nations
even now live without them. But a happy life was not possible
without a clean breast; wherefore with more reason this
man is deemed by us a god, from whom come those sweet
solaces of existence which even now are distributed over great
nations and gently soothe men's minds. Then if you shall
suppose that the deeds of Hercules surpass his, you will
be carried still farther away from true reason. For what
would yon great gaping maw of Nemean lion now harm us
and the bristled Arcadian boar? Ay or what could the bull of
Crete do and the hydra plague of Lerna, fenced round with its
envenomed snakes? Or how could the triple-breasted might of
threefold Geryon, [how could the birds with brazen arrowy
feathers] that dwelt in the Stymphalian swamps do us such
mighty injury, and the horses of Thracian Diomede, breathing
fire from their nostrils along the Bistonian borders and Ismara?
And the serpent which guards the bright golden apples of the
Hesperides, fierce, dangerous of aspect, girding the tree's stem

123

with his enormous body, what harm, pray, could he do us beside the Atlantic shore and melancholy main, which none of us goes near and no barbarian ventures nigh? And all other monsters of the kind which have been destroyed, if they had not been vanquished, what harm could they do, I ask, though now alive? None, methinks: the earth even now so abounds to repletion in wild beasts and is filled with troublous terror throughout woods and great mountains and deep forests; places which we have it for the most part in our own power to shun. But unless the breast is cleared, what battles and dangers must then find their way into us in our own despite; what poignant cares inspired by lust then rend the distressful man, and then also what mighty fears; and pride, filthy lust and wantonness, what disasters they occasion; and luxury and all sorts of sloth! He therefore who shall have subdued all these and banished them from the mind by words, not arms, shall he not have a just title to be ranked among the gods? And all the more so that he was wont to deliver many precepts in beautiful and godlike phrase about the immortal gods themselves and to open up by his teachings all the nature of things.

While walking in his footsteps I follow out his reasonings and teach by my verses, by what law all things are made, what necessity there is then for them to continue in that law, and how impotent they are to annul the binding statutes of time—foremost in which class of things the nature of the mind has been proved to be formed of a body that had birth and to be unable to endure unscathed through great time, mere idols being wont to mock the mind in sleep, when we seem to see him whom life has abandoned. To continue, the order of my design has now brought me to this point, where I must proceed to show that the world is formed of a mortal body and at the same time had birth; to show too in what way that union of matter founded earth, heaven, sea, stars, sun and the ball of the moon; also what living creatures sprang out of the earth, as well as those which never at any time were born; in what way too mankind began to use with one another varied speech by the names conferred on things; and also in what ways yon fear of the gods gained an entry into men's breasts, and now throughout the world maintains as holy fanes, lakes, groves, altars and idols of the gods. Furthermore, I shall make clear by what force piloting nature guides the courses of the sun and the wanderings of the moon; lest haply we imagine that these of their own free will between heaven and earth traverse their everlasting orbits, graciously furthering the increase of crops and living creatures, or we think they roll on by any forethought of the gods. For they who have been rightly taught that the gods lead a life without care, if nevertheless they wonder by what plan all things can be carried on, above all in regard to those things which are seen overhead in the ethereal borders, are borne back again into their old religious scruples and take unto themselves hard taskmasters, whom they, poor wretches, believe to be almighty, not knowing what can, what cannot be, in short by what system each thing has its powers defined, its deep-set boundary mark.

Well then, not to detain you any longer by mere promises, look before all on seas and lands and heaven: their threefold nature, their three bodies, Memmius, three forms so unlike, three such wondrous textures a single day shall give over to destruction; and the mass and fabric of the world upheld for many years shall tumble to ruin. Nor can I fail to perceive with what a novel and strange effect it falls upon the mind, this destruction of heaven and earth that is to be, and how hard it is for me to produce a full conviction of it by words; as is the case when you bring to the ears a thing hitherto unexampled, and yet you cannot submit it to the eyesight nor put it into the hands; through which the straightest highway of belief leads into the human breast and quarters of the mind. But yet I will speak out: it well may be that the reality itself will bring credit to my words and that you will see earthquakes arise and all things grievously shattered to pieces in a short time. But this may pilot fortune guide far away from us, and may reason rather than the reality convince that all things may be overpowered and tumble in with a frightful crash.

But before I shall begin on this question to pour forth decrees of fate with more sanctity and much more certainty than the Pythia who speaks out from the tripod and laurel of Phoebus, I will clearly set forth to you many comforting topics in learned language; lest held in the yoke of religion you haply suppose that earth and sun and heaven, sea, stars, moon must last forever with divine body; and therefore think it right that they after the fashion of the giants should all suffer punishment for their monstrous guilt, who by their reasoning displace the walls of the world and seek to quench the glorious sun of heaven, branding immortal things in mortal speech; though in truth these things are so far from possessing divinity and are so unworthy of being reckoned in the number of gods that they may be thought to afford a notable instance of what is quite without vital motion and sense. For it is quite impossible to suppose that the nature and judgment of the mind can exist with any body whatever; even as a tree cannot exist in the ether nor clouds in the salt sea nor can fishes live in the fields nor blood exist in woods nor sap in stones. Where each thing can grow and abide is fixed and ordained. Thus the nature of the mind cannot come into being alone without the body nor exist far away from the sinews and blood. But if (for this would be much more likely to happen than that) the force itself of the mind might be in the head or shoulders or heels or might be born in any other part of the body, it would after all be wont to abide in one and the same man or vessel. But since in our body even it is fixed and seen to be ordained where the soul and the mind can severally be and grow, it must still more strenuously be denied that it can abide out of the body and the living form altogether in crumbling clods of earth or in the fire of the sun or in water or in the high borders of ether. These things therefore are not possessed of divine sense, since they cannot be quickened with the vital feeling.

This too you may not possibly believe: that the holy seats of the gods exist in any parts of the world. The fine nature of the gods, far withdrawn from our senses, is hardly seen by the thought of the mind; and since it has ever eluded the touch and stroke of the hands, it must touch nothing which is tangible for us; for that cannot touch which does not admit of being touched in turn. And therefore their seats as well must be unlike our seats, must be, to judge from their bodies, exceedingly fine. All which I will prove to you later in copious argument. To say again that for the sake of men they have willed to set in order the glorious nature of the world and therefore it is meet to praise the work of the gods, calling as it does for all praise, and to believe that it will be eternal and immortal, and that it is an unholy thing ever to shake by any force from its fixed seats that which by the forethought of the gods in ancient days has been established on everlasting foundations for mankind, or to assail it by speech and utterly overturn it from top to bottom; and to invent and add other figments of the kind, Memmius, is all sheer folly. For what advantage can our gratitude bestow on immortal and blessed beings, that for our sakes they should take in hand to administer aught? And what novel incident could have induced them, hitherto at rest, so long after to desire to change their former life? But then life, it would seem, lay grovelling in darkness and sorrow, until the first dawn of the birthtime of things; for it seems natural he should rejoice in a new state of things, whom old things annoy; but for him whom no ill has befallen in times gone by, when he passed a pleasant existence, what could have kindled in such a one a love of change? Or what evil had it been for us never to have been born? Whoever has been born must want to continue in life, so long as fond pleasure shall keep him; but for him who has never tasted the love, never been on the lists, of life, what harm not to have been born? Whence again was first implanted in the gods a pattern for begetting things in general as well as the preconception of what men are, so that they knew and saw in mind what they wanted to make; and in what way was the power of first-beginnings ever ascertained, and what they could effect by a change in their mutual arrangements, unless nature herself gave the model for making things? For in suchwise the first-beginnings of things, many in number, in many ways impelled by blows for infinite ages back and kept in motion by their own weights, have been wont to be carried along and to unite in all manner of ways and thoroughly test every kind of production possible by their mutual combinations; that it is not strange if they have also fallen into arrangements and have come into courses like to those out of which this sum of things is now carried on by constant renewing.

But if I did not know what first-beginnings of things are, yet this, judging by the very arrangements of heaven, I would venture to affirm, and led by many other facts to maintain: that the nature of things has by no means been made for us by divine power, so great are the defects with which it is encumbered. In the first place, of all the space which the vast reach of heaven covers, a portion greedy mountains and forests of wild beasts have occupied, rocks and wasteful pools take up, and the sea which holds wide apart the coasts of different lands. Next, of nearly two-thirds burning heat and the constant fall of frost rob mortals. What is left for tillage, even that nature by its power would overrun with thorns, unless the force of man made head against it, accustomed for the sake of a livelihood to groan beneath the strong hoe and to cut through the earth by pressing down the plough. Unless by turning up the fruitful clods with the share and labouring the soil of the earth we stimulate things to rise, they could not spontaneously come up into the clear air; and even then sometimes when things earned with great toil now put forth their leaves over the lands and are all in blossom, either the ethereal sun burns them up with excessive heats or sudden showers and cold frosts cut them off, and the blasts of the winds waste them by a furious hurricane. Again, why does nature give food and increase to the frightful race of wild beasts dangerous to mankind both by sea and land? Why do the seasons of the year bring diseases in their train? Why stalks abroad untimely death? Then too the baby, like to a sailor cast away by the cruel waves, lies naked on the ground, speechless, wanting every furtherance of life, soon as nature by the throes of birth has shed him forth from his mother's womb into the borders of light; he fills the room with a rueful wauling, as well he may whose destiny it is to go through in life so many ills. But the different flocks, herds and wild beasts grow up; they want no rattles; to none of them need be addressed the fond broken accents of the fostering nurse; they ask not different dresses according to the season; no, nor do they want arms or lofty walls, whereby to protect their own, the earth itself and nature manifold in her works producing in plenty all things for all.

First of all, since the body of the earth and water and the light breath of air and burning heats, out of which this sum of things is seen to be formed, do all consist of a body that had a birth and is mortal, the whole nature of the world must be reckoned of a like body. For those things whose parts and members we see to be of a body that had a birth and of forms that are mortal, we perceive to be likewise without exception mortal, and at the same time to have had a birth. Since therefore I see that the chiefest members and parts of the world are destroyed and begotten anew, I may be sure that for heaven and earth as well there has been a time of beginning and there will be a time of destruction.

And herein, that you may not think I have unfairly seized on this point for myself, because I have assumed that earth and fire are mortal and have not doubted that water and air perish, and have said that these are likewise begotten and grow afresh, mark the proofs: first of all, some portion of the earth, burnt up by constant suns, trampled by a multitude of feet, sends forth a cloud and flying eddies of dust, which the strong winds disperse over the whole air. Part too of the soil is put under water by rains, and rivers graze against and eat into the banks. Again, whatever increases something else is in its turn replenished; and since, beyond a doubt, earth the universal mother is found at the same time to be the general tomb of things, therefore you see she is lessened and increases and grows again.

Furthermore, that sea, rivers, fountains always stream over with new moisture and that waters well up without ceasing, it needs no words to prove: the great flow of waters from all sides clearly shows it. But then the water on the surface is always taken off, and thus it is that on the whole there is no overflow, partly because the seas are lessened by the strong winds sweeping over them and by the ethereal sun decomposing them with his rays; partly because the water is diffused below the surface over all lands, for the salt is strained off and the matter of liquid streams back again to the source and all meets together at the riverheads, and then flows over the lands in a fresh current, where a channel once scooped out has carried down the waters with liquid foot.

And next I will speak of the air, which is changed over its whole body every hour in countless ways. For whatever ebbs from things is all borne always into the great sea of air; and unless it in return were to give back bodies to things and to recruit them as they ebb, all things ere now would have been dissolved and changed into air. It therefore ceases not to be begotten from things and to go back again into things, since it is a fact that all things constantly ebb.

Likewise the abundant source of clear light, the ethereal sun, constantly floods heaven with fresh brightness and supplies the place of light on the instant by new light; for every previous emission of brightness is quite lost to it, wherever it falls. This you may know from the following examples: as soon as ever clouds begin to pass below the sun and to break off, so to say, the rays of light, forthwith their lower part is wholly lost, and the earth is overshadowed wherever the clouds pass over; so that you may know that things constantly require new irradiation and that all the preceding emissions of light are lost, and in no other way can things be seen in the sun, unless the fountainhead of light itself send a supply. Moreover, you see, nightly lights which belong to earth, such as hanging lamps and torches bright with darting flames, hasten in like fashion amid great darkness with ministering heat to supply new light; are eager to bicker with fires, eager, I say; nor is the light ever broken off nor does it quit the spots illuminated: with such suddenness from all the fires is its destruction concealed by the swift birth of flame. In the same way then we must believe that sun, moon and stars emit light from fresh and ever fresh supplies rising up, and always lose every previous discharge of flames; that you may not haply believe that these flourish indestructible.

Again, see you not that even stones are conquered by time, that high towers fall and rocks moulder away, that shrines and idols of gods are worn out with decay, and that the holy divinity cannot prolong the bounds of fate or struggle against the fixed laws of nature? Then too see we not the monuments of men fall to ruin, and furthermore brass and solid iron grow old, basalt rocks tumble down, riven away from high mountains and unable to endure and suffer the strong might of finite age? Surely they would never fall, suddenly riven away, if for infinite time past they had held out against all the batteries of age without a crash.

Again, gaze on this, which about and above holds in its embrace all the earth: if it begets all things out of itself, as some say, and takes them back when they are destroyed, then the whole of it has had a birth and is of a mortal body; for whatever gives increase and food out of itself to other things must be lessened; and must be replenished, when it takes things back.

Again, if there was no birth time of earth and heaven and they have been from everlasting, why before the Theban war and the destruction of Troy have not other poets as well sung other themes? Whither have so many deeds of men so often passed away, why live they nowhere embodied in lasting records of fame? The truth, methinks, is that the sun has but a recent date and the nature of the world is new and has but lately had its commencement. Wherefore even now some arts are receiving their last polish, some are even in course of growth; just now many improvements have been made in ships; only yesterday musicians have given birth to tuneful melodies; then too this nature and system of things has been discovered lately, and I the very first of all have only now been found able to transfer it into native words. But if haply you believe that before this all things have existed just the same, but that the generations of men have perished by burning heat, or that cities have fallen by some great concussion of the world, or that after constant rains devouring rivers have gone forth over the earth and have whelmed towns, so much the more you must yield and admit that there will be entire destruction too of earth and heaven, for when things were tried by so great distempers and so great dangers, at that time had a more disastrous cause pressed upon them, they would far and wide have gone to destruction and mighty ruin. And in no other way are we proved to be mortals, except because we all alike in turn fall sick of the same diseases which those had whom nature has withdrawn from life.

Again, whatever things last forever must either, because they are of solid body, repel strokes and not suffer aught to pass into them, sufficient to disunite the closely massed parts within—such are the bodies of matter whose nature we have shown before—or they must be able to endure through all time for this reason; because they are exempt from blows, as void is which remains untouched and suffers not a jot from any stroke; or else because there is no extent of room around, into which things, so to say, may depart and be broken up: in this way the sum of sums is eternal and there is no place outside into which things may spring asunder, nor are there any bodies which can fall upon them and dissolve them by a powerful blow. But the nature of the world, as I have shown, is neither of solid body, since void is mixed up in all things, nor is it again like void, no, nor is there lack of bodies that may haply rise up in mass out of the infinite and overthrow this sum of things with furious tornado or bring upon them some other perilous disaster; nor further is the nature of room and the space of deep void wanting, into which the walls of the world may be scattered abroad; or they may be assailed and perish by some other force. Therefore the gate of death is not closed against heaven or sun or earth or deep waters of the sea, but stands open and looks towards them with a huge wide-gaping maw. And therefore also you must admit that these things likewise had a birth; for things which are of mortal body could not for an infinite time back up to the present have been able to set at naught the puissant strength of immeasurable age.

Again, since the chiefest members of the world fight so hotly together, fiercely stirred by no hallowed civil warfare, see you not that some limit may be set to their long struggle, either when the sun and all heat shall have drunk up all the waters and gotten the mastery: this they are ever striving to do, but as yet are unable to accomplish their endeavours, such abundant supplies the rivers furnish, and threaten to turn aggressors and flood all things with a deluge from the deep gulf of ocean—all in vain, since the winds sweeping over the seas and the ethereal sun decomposing them with his rays do lessen them, and trust to be able to dry all things up before water can attain the end of its endeavour. Such a war do they breathe out with undecided issue, and strive with each other to determine it for mighty ends; though once by the way fire got the upper hand and once, as the story goes, water reigned dominant in the fields. Fire gained the mastery and licked and burnt up many things, when the headstrong might of the horses of the sun dashed from the course and hurried Phaëthon through the whole sky and over all lands. But the almighty father then, stirred to fierce wrath, with a sudden thunderstroke dashed Phaëthon down from his horses to earth, and the sun, meeting him as he fell, caught from him the everburning lamp of the world and got in hand the scattered steeds and yoked them, shaking all over; then guided them on his proper course and gave fresh life to all things. Thus, to wit, have the old poets of the Greeks sung; though it is all too widely at variance with true reason. Fire may gain the mastery when more bodies of matter than usual have gathered themselves up out of the infinite; and then its powers decay, vanquished in some way or other, or else things perish, burnt up by the torrid air. Water too of yore gathered itself and began to get the mastery, as the story goes, when it whelmed many cities of men; and then when all that force that had gathered itself up out of the infinite, by some means or other was turned aside and withdrew, the rains were stayed and the rivers abated their fury.

But in what ways yon concourse of matter founded earth and heaven and the deeps of the sea, the courses of sun and moon, I will next in order describe. For verily not by design

did the first-beginnings of things station themselves each in its
right place by keen-sighted intelligence, nor did they bargain,
sooth to say, what motions each should assume, but because
the first-beginnings of things, many in number, in many ways
impelled by blows for infinite ages back and kept in motion by
their own weights, have been wont to be carried along and to
unite in all manner of ways and thoroughly to test every kind
of production possible by their mutual combinations, therefore
it is that, spread abroad through great time after trying unions
and motions of every kind, they at length meet together in
those masses which, suddenly brought together, become often
the rudiments of great things, of earth, sea and heaven and
the race of living things.

At this time then neither could the sun's disk be discerned
flying aloft with its abundant light, nor the stars of great ether,
nor sea nor heaven, no, nor earth nor air, nor could anything
be seen like to our things, but only a strange stormy crisis and
medley, gathered together out of first-beginnings of every
kind, whose state of discord, joining battle, disordered their
interspaces, passages, connexions, weights, blows, clashings,
motions, because by reason of their unlike forms and varied
shapes they could not all remain thus joined together nor fall
into mutually harmonious motions. Then next the several parts
began to fly asunder and things to be joined like with like and
to mark off the world and portion out its members and arrange
its mighty parts, that is to say, to separate high heaven from
earth, and let the sea spread itself out apart with its unmixed
water, and likewise let the fires of ether spread apart pure and
unmixed.

For first the several bodies of earth, because they were
heavy and closely entangled, met together in the middle and
took up all of them the lowest positions; and the more they
got entangled and the closer their union, the more they
squeezed out those particles which were to make up sea, stars,
sun and moon and the walls of the great world. All these are of
smooth and round seeds and of much smaller elements than the
earth. Therefore the fire-laden ether first burst out from the
different parts of the earth through all the porous openings
and lightly bore off with itself many fires; much in the same
way as we often see, so soon as the morning light of the
beaming sun blushes golden over the grass jewelled with dew,
and the pools and the ever-running rivers exhale a mist, and

even as the earth itself is sometimes seen to smoke; and when all these are gathered together aloft, then do clouds on high with a now cohering body weave a covering beneath heaven. In this way therefore then the light and expansive ether with its now cohering body swept round and arched itself on all sides, and expanding widely in all directions round in this way, fenced all other things in with its greedy grasp. After it followed the rudiments of sun and moon, whose spheres turn round in air midway between earth and ether: these neither earth has taken unto itself nor greatest ether, because they were neither heavy enough to sink and settle down nor light enough to glide along the uppermost borders; they yet, however, are so placed between the two as to wheel along their lifelike bodies and still to be parts of the whole world; just as in us some members may be at rest, while others at the same time are in motion. These things then being withdrawn, the earth, in those parts where the vast azure level of ocean now spreads, in a moment sank in and drenched with salt flood the hollows. And every day the more the heats of ether round and the rays of the sun on all sides compressed the earth into a close mass by oft-repeated blows on all its outer edges, so that thus buffeted it was condensed and drawn together about its centre, ever the more did the salt sweat squeezed out of its body increase by its oozings the sea and floating fields, and ever the more did those many bodies of heat and air escape and fly abroad and condense far away from earth the high glittering quarters of heaven. The plains sank down, the high hills grew in elevation; for the rocks could not settle down nor all the parts sink to one uniform level.

Thus then the ponderous mass of earth was formed with close-cohering body and all the slime of the world, so to speak, slid down by its weight to the lowest point and settled at the bottom like dregs. Then the sea, then the air, then the fire-laden ether itself, all are left unmixed with their clear bodies; and some are lighter than others, and clearest and lightest of all, ether floats upon the airy currents, and blends not its clear body with the troubled airs; it suffers all these things below to be upset with furious hurricanes, suffers them to be troubled by wayward storms; while it carries along its own fires gliding with a changeless onward sweep. For that ether may stream on gently and with one uniform effort the Pontos shows, a sea which streams with a changeless current, ever preserving one uniform gliding course.

Let us now sing what causes the motions of the stars. In the first place, if the great sphere of heaven revolves, we must say that an air presses on the pole at each end and confines it on the outside and closes it in at both ends; and then that a third air streams above and moves in the same direction in which roll on as they shine the stars of the eternal world; or else that this third air streams below in order to carry up the sphere in the contrary direction; just as we see rivers turn wheels and water scoops. It is likewise quite possible too that all the heaven remains at rest, while at the same time the glittering signs are carried on; either because rapid heats of ether are shut in and whirl round while seeking a way out and roll their fires in all directions through heaven's vast quarters; or else an air streaming from some part from another source outside drives and whirls the fires; or else they may glide on of themselves, going whithersoever the food of each calls and invites them, feeding their flamy bodies everywhere throughout heaven. For which of these causes is in operation in this world, it is not easy to affirm for certain; but what can be and is done throughout the universe in various worlds formed on various plans, this I teach, and I go on to set forth several causes which may exist throughout the universe for the motions of stars; one of which, however, must in this world also be the cause that imparts lively motion to the signs; but to dictate which of them it is, is by no means the duty of the man who advances step by step.

And in order that the earth may rest in the middle of the world, it is proper that its weight should gradually pass away and be lessened, and that it should have another nature underneath it conjoined from the beginning of its existence and formed into one being with the airy portions of the world in which it is embodied and lives. For this reason it is no burden and does not weigh down the air; just as his limbs are of no weight to a man nor is his head a burden to his neck, nor do we feel that the whole weight of the body rests on the feet; but whatever weights come from without and are laid upon us hurt us, though they are often very much smaller: of such great moment it is what function each thing has to perform. Thus then the earth is not an alien body suddenly brought in and forced from some other quarter on air alien to it, but was conceived together with it at the first birth of the world and is a fixed portion of that world, just as our limbs are seen to be to us. Again, the earth when suddenly shaken by loud thunder shakes by its motion all the things which are above it; and this it could in no wise do, unless it had been fast bound with the airy portions of the world and with heaven. For the earth and they cohere with one another by common roots, conjoined and formed into a single being from the beginning of their existence. See you not too that great as is the weight of our body, the force of the soul, though of the extremest fineness, supports it, because it is so closely conjoined and formed into a single being with it? Then too, what is able to lift the body with a nimble bound save the force of the mind which guides the limbs? Now do you see what power a subtle nature may have, when it is conjoined with a heavy body, as the air is conjoined with the earth and the force of the mind with us?

Again, the disk of the sun cannot be much larger, nor its body of heat much smaller, than they appear to be to our senses. For from whatever distances fires can reach us with their light and breathe on our limbs burning heat, those distances take away nothing by such spaces between from the body of the flames, the fire is not in the least narrowed in appearance. Therefore, since the heat of the sun and the light which it sheds reach our senses and stroke the proper places, the form too and size of the sun must be seen from this earth in their real dimensions, so that you may not add anything whatever more or less. And whether the moon as it is borne on illuminates places with a borrowed light, or emits its own light from its own body, whatever that is, the form with which it is thus borne on is not at all larger than the one which it presents to our eyes seems to us to be. For all things which we see at a great distance through much air look dimmed in appearance before their size is diminished. Therefore since the moon presents a bright aspect and well-defined form, it must be seen on high by us from this earth precisely as it is in the outline which defines it, and of the size it actually is. Lastly, in the case of all those fires of ether which you observe from this earth—since in the case of fires which we see here on earth, so long as their flickering is distinct, so long as their heat is perceived, their size is seen sometimes to change to a very, very small extent either way, according to the distance at which they are—you may infer that the fires of ether may be smaller than they look in an extremely minute degree, or larger by a very small and insignificant fraction.

This likewise need not excite wonder: how it is that so small a body as yon sun can emit so great a light, enough to flood completely seas and all lands and heaven and to steep all things in its burning heat. It well may be that a single spring for the whole world may open up from this spot and gush out in plenteous stream and shoot forth light, because elements of heat meet together from all sides out of the whole world in such manner, and the mass of them thrown together streams to a point in such manner, that this heat wells forth from a single source. See you not too what a breadth of meadowland a small spring of water sometimes floods, streaming out over the fields? It is likewise possible that heat from the sun's flame though not at all great may infect the whole air with fervent fires, if haply the air is in a suitable and susceptible state, so that it can be kindled when struck by small bodies of heat; thus we see sometimes a general conflagration from a single spark catch fields of corn and stubble. Perhaps too the sun as he shines aloft with rosy lamp has round about him much fire with heats that are not visible, and thus the fire may be marked by no radiance, so that, fraught with heat, it increases to such a degree the stroke of the rays.

Nor with regard to the sun is there one single explanation, certain and manifest, of the way in which he passes from his summer positions to the midwinter turning point of Capricorn and then turning back from thence bends his course to the solstitial goal of Cancer, and how the moon is seen once a month to pass over that space in traversing which the sun spends the period of a year. No single plain cause, I say, has been assigned for these things. It seems highly probable that that may be the truth which the revered judgment of the worthy man Democritus maintains: the nearer the different constellations are to the earth, the less they can be carried along with the whirl of heaven; for the velocity of its force, he says, passes away and the intensity diminishes in the lower parts, and therefore the sun is gradually left behind with the rearward signs, because he is much lower than the burning signs. And the moon more than the sun: the lower her path is and the more distant she is from heaven and the nearer she approaches to earth, the less she can keep pace with the signs. For the fainter the whirl is in which she is borne along, being as she is lower than the sun, so much the more all the signs around overtake and pass her. Therefore it is that she appears to come back to every sign more quickly, because the signs go more quickly back to her. It is quite possible too that from quarters of the world crossing the sun's path two airs may stream each in its turn at a fixed time; one of which may force the sun away from the summer signs so far as his midwinter turning point and freezing cold, and the other may force him back from the freezing shades of cold as far as the heat-laden quarters and burning signs. And in like manner we must suppose that the moon, and the stars which make revolutions of great years in great orbits, may pass by means of airs from opposite quarters in turn. See you not too that clouds from contrary winds pass in contrary directions, the upper in a contrary way to the lower? Why may not yon stars just as well be borne on through their great orbits in ether by currents contrary one to the other?

But night buries the earth in thick darkness, either when the sun after his long course has struck upon the utmost parts of heaven and now exhausted has blown forth all his fires shaken by their journey and weakened by passing through much air; or else because the same force which has carried on his orb above the earth compels him to change his course and pass below the earth.

At a fixed time too Matuta spreads rosy morning over the borders of ether and opens up her light, either because the same sun coming back below the earth, seizes heaven before his time trying to kindle it with his rays; or because fires meet together and many seeds of heat are accustomed to stream together at a fixed time, which cause new sunlight to be born every day. Thus they tell that from the high mountains of Ida scattered fires are seen at daybreak, that these then unite, as it were, into a single ball and make up an orb. And herein it ought to cause no surprise that these seeds of fire stream together at a time so surely fixed and reproduce the radiance of the sun. For we see many occurrences which take place at a fixed time in all things. At a fixed time trees blossom and at a fixed time shed their blossoms; and at a time no less surely fixed age bids the teeth be shed and the boy put on the soft dress of puberty and let a soft beard fall down equally from each cheek. Lastly, lightnings, snow, rains, clouds, winds take place at not very irregular seasons of year. For where causes from their very first beginnings have been in this way and things have thus fallen out from the first birth of the world, in due sequence too they now come round after a fixed order.

Likewise days may lengthen and nights wane, and days shorten when the nights receive increase, either because the same sun, running his course below the earth and above in curves of unlike length, parts the borders of ether and divides his orbit into unequal halves; and as he comes round adds on in the opposite half just as much as he has subtracted from the other of the two halves, until he has arrived at that sign of heaven where the node of the year makes the shades of night of the same length as the daylight. For when the sun's course lies midway between the blast of the north and of the south, heaven keeps his two goals apart at distances now rendered exactly equal on account of the position of the whole starry circle, in gliding through which the sun takes up the period of a year, lighting with slanting rays earth and heaven; as is clearly shown by the plans of those who have mapped out all the quarters of heaven as they are set off with their array of signs. Or else because the air is denser in certain parts, therefore the quivering beam of fire is retarded below the earth and cannot easily pass through and force its way out to its place of rising: for this reason in wintertime nights linger long, ere the beamy badge of day arrive. Or else, because in the way just mentioned at alternate parts of the year fires are accustomed to stream together more slowly and more quickly, which cause the sun to rise in a certain point, therefore it is that those appear to speak the truth [who suppose a fresh sun to be born every day].

The moon may shine because struck by the sun's rays, and turn that light every day more and more directly towards our sight, in proportion as she recedes from the sun's orb, until just opposite to him she has shone out with full light and at her rising as she soars aloft has beheld his setting; and then by slow steps reversing, as it were, her course, she must in the same way hide her light, the nearer and nearer she now glides to the sun from a different quarter through the circle of the signs; according to the theory of those who suppose the moon to be like a ball and to hold on her course under the sun. She may also very possibly revolve with her own light and display various phases of brightness; for there may well be another body which is carried on and glides in her company, getting before her path and obstructing her in all manner of ways and yet cannot be seen, because it glides on without light. She may also revolve, like it may be to a spherical ball steeped over one half in shining light, and as she rolls round this sphere she may present changing phases, until she has turned that half which is illuminated full towards our sight and open eyes; then by slow steps she whirls back and withdraws the light-fraught half of the spherical ball; as the Babylonian science of the Chaldees refuting the system of the astronomers essays to prove in opposition to them; just as though that which each party fights for might not be equally true, or there were any reason why you should venture to embrace the one theory less than the other. Again, why a new moon should not be born every day after a regular succession of forms and regular phases, and each day the one which is born perish and another be produced in its room and stead, it is not easy to teach by reasoning or prove by words, since so many things can be born in such a regular succession. Spring and Venus go their way, and spring's harbinger, winged zephyr, steps on before; and along the path they tread mother Flora straws all the way before them and covers it over with the choicest colours and odours. Next in order follows parching heat and in its company dusty Ceres and the etesian blasts of the north winds. Next autumn advances and Euhius Euan steps on together. Then other seasons and winds follow, loud-roaring Volturnus and the south wind, stored with lightning. At last midwinter brings with it snows and benumbing cold; winter goes forth; after it follows cold chattering with its teeth. It is therefore the less strange that a moon is begotten at a fixed time and at a fixed time is destroyed again, since many things may take place at a time so surely fixed.

The eclipses of the sun likewise and the obscurations of the moon you may suppose to take place from many different causes. For why should the moon be able to shut the earth out from the sun's light and keep off from the earth his high-exalted head, placing her dark orb before his burning rays; and yet at the same time it be thought that another body gliding on ever without light cannot do the same? Why too should not the sun be able, quite exhausted, to lose his fires at a fixed time, and again reproduce his light when in his journey through the air he has passed by spots fatal to his flames, which cause his fires to be quenched and to perish? And why should the earth be able to turn to rob the moon of light and moreover herself to keep the sun suppressed, while in her monthly course she glides through the well-defined shadows of the cone; and yet at the same time another body not be able to pass under the moon or glide above the sun's orb, breaking off its rays and the light it sheds forth? Yes and if the moon shines with her own brightness, why should she not be able to grow faint in a certain part of the world, while she is passing through spots hostile to her own light.

And now further, since I have explained in what way everything might take place throughout the blue of the great heaven —how we might know what force and cause set in motion the varied courses of the sun and wanderings of the moon; and in what way their light might be intercepted and they be lost to us and spread darkness over the earth little expecting it, when, so to speak, they close their eye of light and, opening it again, survey all places shining in bright radiance—I now go back to the infancy of the world and the tender age of the fields of earth and show what first in their early essays of production they resolved to raise into the borders of light and to give in charge to the wayward winds.

In the beginning the earth gave forth all kinds of herbage and verdant sheen about the hills and over all the plains; the flowery meadows glittered with the bright green hue, and next in order to the different trees was given a strong and emulous desire of growing up into the air with full unbridled powers. As feathers and hairs and bristles are first born on the limbs of four-footed beasts and the body of the strong of wing, thus the new earth then first put forth grass and bushes, and next gave birth to the races of mortal creatures springing up many in number in many ways after divers fashions. For no living creatures can have dropped from heaven, nor can those belonging to the land have come out of the salt pools. It follows that with good reason the earth has gotten the name of mother, since all things have been produced out of the earth. And many living creatures even now spring out of the earth, taking form by rains and the heat of the sun. It is therefore the less strange if at that time they sprang up more in number and larger in size, having come to maturity in the infancy of earth and ether. First of all the race of fowls and the various birds would leave their eggs, hatched in the springtime, just as now in summer the cicadas leave spontaneously their delicate coats in quest of a living and life. Then, you must know, did the earth first give forth races of mortal men. For much heat and moisture would then abound in the fields; and therefore wherever a suitable spot offered, wombs would grow attached to the earth by roots; and when the warmth of the infants, flying the wet and craving the air, had opened these in the fullness of time, nature would turn to that spot the pores of the earth and constrain it to yield from its opened veins a liquid most like to milk, even as nowadays every woman when she has borne is filled with sweet milk, because all that current of nutriment streams towards the breasts. To the children the earth would furnish food, the heat raiment, the grass a bed rich in abundance of soft down. Then the fresh youth of the world would give forth neither severe colds nor excessive heats nor gales of great violence; for all things grow and acquire strength in a like proportion.

Wherefore again and again I say the earth with good title has gotten and keeps the name of mother, since she of herself gave birth to mankind and at a time nearly fixed shed forth every beast that ranges wildly over the great mountains, and at the same time the fowls of the air with all their varied shapes. But because she must have some limit set to her bearing, she ceased like a woman worn out by length of days. For time changes the nature of the whole world and all things must pass on from one condition to another, and nought continues like to itself: all things quit their bounds, all things nature changes and compels to alter. One thing crumbles away and is worn and enfeebled with age, then another comes unto honour and issues out of its state of contempt. In this way then time changes the nature of the whole world and the earth passes out of one condition into another, so that now it cannot bear what once it could, and now it can bear what before it did not bear.

And many monsters too the earth at that time essayed to produce, things coming up with strange face and limbs, the man-woman, a thing between the two and neither the one sex nor the other, widely differing from both; some things deprived of feet, others again destitute of hands, others too proving dumb without mouth, or blind without eyes, and things bound fast by the adhesion of their limbs over all the body, so that they could not do anything nor go anywhere nor avoid the evil nor take what their needs required. Every other monster and portent of this kind she would produce, but all in vain, since nature set a ban on their increase and they could not reach the coveted flower of age nor find food nor be united in marriage. For we see that many conditions must meet together in things in order that they may beget and continue their kinds; first a supply of food, then a way by which the birth-producing seeds throughout the frame may stream from the relaxed limbs; also in order that the woman may be united with the male, the possession of organs whereby they may each interchange mutual joys.

And many races of living things must then have died out and been unable to beget and continue their breed. For in the case of all things which you see breathing the breath of life, either craft or courage or else speed has from the beginning of its existence protected and preserved each particular race. And there are many things which, recommended to us by their useful services, continue to exist consigned to our protection. In the first place, the fierce breed of lions and the savage races their courage has protected, foxes their craft and stags their proneness to flight. But light-sleeping dogs with faithful heart in breast and every kind which is born of the seed of beasts of burden and at the same time the woolly flocks and the horned herds are all consigned, Memmius, to the protection of man. For they have ever fled with eagerness from wild beasts and have ensued peace, and plenty of food has been obtained without their own labour, as we give it in requital of their useful services. But those to whom nature has granted none of these qualities, so that they could neither live by their own means nor perform for us any useful service in return for which we should suffer their kind to feed and be safe under our protection, those, you are to know, would lie exposed as a prey and booty of others, hampered all in their own death-bringing shackles, until nature brought that kind to utter destruction.

But centaurs never have existed, and at no time can there exist things of twofold nature and double body formed into one frame out of limbs of alien kinds, such that the faculties and powers of this and that portion cannot be sufficiently like. This, however dull of understanding, you may learn from what follows. To begin, a horse when three years have gone round is in the prime of his vigour, far different the boy:

often even at that age he will call in his sleep for the milk of the breast. Afterwards when in advanced age his lusty strength and limbs, now faint from ebbing life, fail the horse, then and not till then youth in the flower of age commences for that boy and clothes his cheeks in soft down; that you may not haply believe that out of a man and the burden-carrying seed of horses centaurs can be formed and have being; or that Scyllas with bodies half those of fishes girdled round with raving dogs can exist, and all other things of the kind, whose limbs we see cannot harmonise together; as they neither come to their flower at the same time nor reach the fullness of their bodily strength nor lose it in advanced old age, nor burn with similar passions nor have compatible manners, nor feel the same things give pleasure throughout their frames. Thus we may see bearded goats often fatten on hemlock, which for man is rank poison. Since flame, moreover, is wont to scorch and burn the tawny bodies of lions just as much as any other kind of flesh and blood existing on earth, how could it be that a single chimera with triple body, in front a lion, behind a dragon, in the middle the goat whose name it bears, could breathe out at the mouth fierce flame from its body? Wherefore also he who fables that in the new time of the earth and the fresh youth of heaven such living creatures could have been begotten, resting upon this one futile term "new," may babble out many things in like fashion, may say that rivers then ran with gold over all parts of the earth, and that trees were wont to blossom with precious stones, or that man was born with such giant force of frame that he could wade on foot across deep seas and whirl the whole heaven about him with his hands. For the fact that there were many seeds of things in the earth what time it first shed forth living creatures is yet no proof that there could have been produced beasts of different kinds mixed together, and limbs of different living things formed into a single frame, because the kinds of herbage and corn and joyous trees which even now spring in plenty out of the earth yet cannot be produced with the several sorts plaited into one, but each thing goes on after its own fashion, and all preserve their distinctive differences according to a fixed law of nature.

But the race of man then in the fields was much hardier, as beseemed it to be, since the hard earth had produced it; and built on a groundwork of larger and more solid bones within, knit with powerful sinews throughout the frame of flesh; not lightly to be disabled by heat or cold or strange kinds of food or any malady of body. And during the revolution of many lustres of the sun through heaven, they led a life after the roving fashion of wild beasts. No one then was a sturdy guider of the bent plough or knew how to labour the fields with iron or plant in the ground young saplings or lop with pruning hooks old boughs from the high trees. What the sun and rains had given, what the earth had produced spontaneously, was guerdon sufficient to content their hearts. Among acorn-bearing oaks they would refresh their bodies for the most part; and the arbute berries which you now see in the wintertime ripen with a bright scarlet hue, the earth would then bear in greatest plenty and of a larger size; and many coarse kinds of food besides the teeming freshness of the world then bare, more than enough for poor wretched men. But rivers and springs invited to slake thirst, even as now a rush of water down from the great hills summons with clear plash far and wide the thirsty races of wild beasts. Then too as they ranged about they would occupy the well-known woodland haunts of the nymphs, out of which they knew that smooth-gliding streams of water with a copious gush bathed the dripping rocks, the dripping rocks, trickling down over the green moss; and in parts welled and bubbled out over the level plain. And as yet they knew not how to apply fire to their purposes or to make use of skins and clothe their body in the spoils of wild beasts, but they would dwell in woods and mountain caves and forests and shelter in the brushwood their squalid limbs when driven to shun the buffeting of the winds and the rains. And they were unable to look to the general weal and knew not how to make a common use of any customs or laws. Whatever prize fortune threw in his way, each man would bear off, trained at his own discretion to think of himself and live for himself alone. And Venus would join the bodies of lovers in the woods; for each woman was gained over either by mutual desire or the headstrong violence and vehement lust of the man or a bribe of some acorns and arbute berries or choice pears. And trusting to the marvellous powers of their hands and feet, they would pursue the forest-haunting races of wild beasts with showers of stones and club of ponderous weight; and many they would conquer, a few they would avoid in hiding places; and like to bristly swine, just as they were they would throw their savage limbs all naked on the ground, when overtaken by night, covering themselves up with leaves and boughs. Yet never with loud wailings would they call for the daylight and the sun, wandering terror-stricken over the fields in the shadows of night, but silent and buried in sleep they would wait, till the sun with rosy torch carried light into heaven; for accustomed as they had been from childhood always to see darkness and light begotten time about, never could any wonder come over them, nor any misgiving that never-ending night would cover the earth and the light of the sun be withdrawn for evermore. But what gave them trouble was rather the races of wild beasts which would often render repose fatal to the poor wretches. And driven from their home they would fly from their rocky shelters on the approach of a foaming boar or a strong lion, and in the dead of night they would surrender in terror to their savage guests their sleeping places strawn with leaves.

Nor then much more than now would the races of mortal men leave the sweet light of ebbing life. For then this one or that other one of them would be more likely to be seized, and torn open by their teeth, would furnish to the wild beasts a living food, and would fill with his moaning woods and mountains and forests as he looked on his living flesh buried in a living grave. But those whom flight had saved with body eaten into, holding ever after their quivering palms over the noisome sores would summon death with appalling cries, until cruel gripings had rid them of life, forlorn of help, unwitting what wounds wanted. But then a single day gave not over to death many thousands of men marching with banners spread, nor did the stormy waters of the sea dash on the rocks men and ships. At this time the sea would often rise up and rage without aim, without purpose, without result, and just as lightly put off its empty threats; nor could the winning wiles of the calm sea treacherously entice anyone to his ruin with laughing waters. Then too want of food would consign to death their fainting frames, now on the contrary 'tis plenty sinks into ruin. They unwittingly would often pour out poison for themselves; now with nicer skill men give it to their son's wife instead.

Next after they had got themselves huts and skins and fire, and the woman united with the man passed into the bonds of marriage with one, and they saw an offspring born from them, then first mankind began to soften. For fire made their chilled bodies less able now to bear the frost beneath the canopy of heaven, and Venus impaired their strength and children with their caresses soon broke down the haughty temper of parents. Then too neighbours began to join in a league of friendship mutually desiring neither to do nor suffer harm; and asked for indulgence to children and womankind, when with cries and gestures they declared in stammering speech that meet it is for all to have mercy on the weak. And though harmony could not be established without exception, yet a very large portion observed their agreements with good faith, or else the race of man would then have been wholly cut off, nor could the breed have continued their generations to this day.

But nature impelled them to utter the various sounds of the tongue and use struck out the names of things, much in the same way as the inability to speak is seen in its turn to drive children to the use of gestures, when it forces them to point with the finger at the things which are before them. For every-one feels how far he can make use of his peculiar powers. Ere the horns of a calf are formed and project from his forehead, he butts with it when angry and pushes out in his rage. Then whelps of panthers and cubs of lions fight with claws and feet and teeth at a time when teeth and claws are hardly yet formed. Again we see every kind of fowl trust to wings and seek from pinions a fluttering succour. Therefore to suppose that some one man at that time apportioned names to things and that men from him learnt their first words is sheer folly. For why should this particular man be able to denote all things by words and to utter the various sounds of the tongue, and yet at the same time others be supposed not to have been able to do so? Again, if others as well as he had not made use of words among themselves, whence was implanted in this man the previous conception of its use and whence was given to him the original faculty, to know and perceive in mind what he wanted to do? Again, one man could not constrain and subdue and force many to choose to learn the names of things. It is no easy thing in any way to teach and convince the deaf of what is needful to be done; for they never would suffer nor in any way endure sounds of voice hitherto unheard to continue to be dinned fruitlessly into their ears. Lastly, what is there so passing strange in this circumstance, that the race of men, whose voice and tongue were in full force, should denote things by different words as different feelings prompted, since dumb brutes, yes and the races of wild beasts, are accustomed to give forth distinct and varied sounds, when they have fear or pain and when joys are rife. This you may learn from facts plain to sense: when the large spongy opened lips of Molossian dogs begin to growl enraged and bare their hard teeth, thus drawn back in rage they threaten in a tone far different from that in which they bark outright and fill with sounds all the places round. Again, when they essay fondly to lick their whelps with their tongue or when they toss them with their feet and snapping at them make a feint, with lightly closing teeth, of swallowing, though with gentle forbearance, they caress them with a yelping sound of a sort greatly differing from that which they utter when, left alone in a house, they bay or when they slink away howling from blows with a crouching body. Again, is not the neigh too seen to differ, when a young stallion in the flower of age rages among the mares smitten by the goads of winged love, and when with wide-stretched nostrils he snorts out the signal to arms, and when as it chances on any other occasion he neighs with limbs all shaking? Lastly, the race of fowls and various birds, hawks and ospreys and gulls, seeking their living in the salt water mid the waves of the sea, utter at a different time noises widely differing from those they make when they are fighting for food and struggling with their prey. And some of them change together with the weather their harsh croakings, as the long-lived races of crows and flocks of rooks when they are said to be calling for water and rain and sometimes to be summoning winds and gales. Therefore if different sensations compel creatures, dumb though they be, to utter different sounds, how much more natural it is that mortal men in those times should have been able to denote dissimilar things by many different words!

And lest haply on this head you ask in silent thought this question, it was lightning that brought fire down on earth for mortals in the beginning; thence the whole heat of flames is spread abroad. Thus we see many things shine, dyed in heavenly flames, when the stroke from heaven has stored them with its heat. Ay and without this, when a branching tree sways to and fro and tosses about under the buffeting of the winds, pressing against the boughs of another tree, fire is forced out by the power of the violent friction, and sometimes the burning heat of flame flashes out, the boughs and stems rubbing against each other. Now either of these accidents may have given fire to men. Next the sun taught them to cook food and soften it with the heat of flame, since they would see many things grow mellow, when subdued by the strokes of the rays and by heat throughout the fields.

And more and more every day men who excelled in intellect and were of vigorous understanding would kindly show them how to exchange their former way of living for new methods. Kings began to build towns and lay out a citadel as a place of strength and of refuge for themselves, and divided cattle and lands and gave to each man in proportion to his personal beauty and strength and intellect; for beauty and vigorous strength were much esteemed. Afterwards wealth was discovered and gold found out, which soon robbed of their honours strong and beautiful alike; for men however valiant and beautiful of person generally follow in the train of the richer man. But were a man to order his life by the rules of true reason, a frugal subsistence joined to a contented mind is for him great riches; for never is there any lack of a little. But men desire to be famous and powerful, in order that their fortunes might rest on a firm foundation and they might be able by their wealth to lead a tranquil life; but in vain, since in their struggle to mount up to the highest dignities they rendered their path one full of danger; and even if they reach it, yet envy like a thunderbolt sometimes strikes and dashes men down from the highest point with ignominy into noisome Tartarus; since the highest summits and those elevated above the level of other things are mostly blasted by envy as by a thunderbolt; so that far better it is to obey in peace and quiet than to wish to rule with power supreme and be the master of kingdoms. Therefore let men wear themselves out to no purpose and sweat drops of blood, as they struggle on along the strait road of ambition, since they gather their knowledge from the mouths of others and follow after things from hearsay rather than the dictates of their own feelings; and this prevails not now nor will prevail by and by any more than it has prevailed before.

Kings therefore being slain, the old majesty of thrones and proud sceptres were overthrown and laid in the dust, and the glorious badge of the sovereign head, bloodstained beneath the feet of the rabble, mourned for its high prerogative; for that is greedily trampled on which before was too much dreaded. Power therefore would fall to the lowest dregs and to unruly mobs, each man seeking for himself empire and sovereignty. Then a portion of them taught men to elect legal officers, and drew up codes, to induce men to obey the laws. For mankind, tired out with a life of brute force, lay exhausted from its feuds; and therefore the more readily it submitted of its own free will to laws and stringent codes. For as each one, moved by anger, took measures to avenge himself with more severity than is now permitted by equitable laws, for this reason men grew sick of a life of brute force. Thence fear of punishment mars the prizes of life; for violence and wrong enclose all who commit them in their meshes and do mostly recoil on him from whom they began; and it is not easy for him who by his deeds transgresses the terms of the public peace to pass a tranquil and a peaceful existence. For though he eludes God and man, yet he cannot but feel a misgiving that his secret can be kept forever; seeing that many by speaking in their dreams or in the wanderings of disease have often, we are told, betrayed themselves and have disclosed their hidden deeds of evil and their sins.

And now what cause has spread over great nations the worship of the divinities of the gods and filled towns with altars and led to the performance of stated sacred rites, rites now in fashion on solemn occasions and in solemn places, from which even now is implanted in mortals a shuddering awe which raises new temples of the gods over the whole earth and prompts men to crowd them on festive days—all this it is not so difficult to explain in words. Even then in sooth the races of mortal men would see in waking mind glorious forms, would see them in sleep of yet more marvellous size of body. To these then they would attribute sense, because they seemed to move their limbs and to utter lofty words suitable to their glorious aspect and surpassing powers. And they would give them life everlasting, because their face would ever appear before them and their form abide; yes and yet without all this, because they would not believe that beings possessed of such powers could lightly be overcome by any force. And they would believe them to be pre-eminent in bliss, because none of them was ever troubled with the fear of death, and because at the same time in sleep they would see them perform many

miracles, yet feel on their part no fatigue from the effort.
Again, they would see the system of heaven and the different
seasons of the years come round in regular succession, and
could not find out by what causes this was done; therefore
they would seek a refuge in handling over all things to the
gods and supposing all things to be guided by their nod. And
they placed in heaven the abodes and realms of the gods,
because night and moon are seen to roll through heaven,
moon, day and night and night's austere constellations and
night-wandering meteors of the sky and flying bodies of
flame, clouds, sun, rains, snow, winds, lightnings, hail and
rapid rumblings and loud threatful thunderclaps.

O hapless race of men, when that they charged the gods
with such acts and coupled with them bitter wrath! What
groanings did they then beget for themselves, what wounds for
us, what tears for our children's children! No act is it of piety
to be often seen with veiled head to turn to a stone and approach every altar and fall prostrate on the ground and spread
out the palms before the statues of the gods and sprinkle the
altars with much blood of beasts and nail up vow after vow,
but rather to be able to look on all things with a mind at
peace. For when we turn our gaze on the heavenly quarters
of the great upper world and ether fast above the glittering
stars, and direct our thoughts to the courses of the sun and
moon, then into our breasts burdened with other ills that fear
as well begins to exalt its reawakened head, the fear that we
may haply find the power of the gods to be unlimited, able
to wheel the bright stars in their varied motion; for lack of
power to solve the question troubles the mind with doubts,
whether there was ever a birth time of the world, and whether
likewise there is to be any end; how far the walls of the world
can endure this strain of restless motion; or whether, gifted by
the grace of the gods with an everlasting existence, they may
glide on through a never-ending tract of time and defy the
strong powers of immeasurable ages. Again, who is there
whose mind does not shrink into itself with fear of the gods,
whose limbs do not cower in terror, when the parched earth
rocks with the appalling stroke and rattlings run through the
great heaven? Do not peoples and nations quake, and proud
monarchs shrink into themselves smitten with fear of the gods,
lest for any foul transgression or overweening word the heavy
time of reckoning has arrived at its fullness? When too the ut-

most fury of the headstrong wind passes over the sea and sweeps over its waters the commander of a fleet together with his mighty legions and elephants, does he not draw near with vows to seek the mercy of the gods and ask in prayer with fear and trembling a lull in the winds and propitious gales; but all in vain, since often, caught up in the furious hurricane, he is borne none the less to the shoals of death? So constantly does some hidden power trample on human grandeur and is seen to tread under its heel and make sport for itself of the renowned rods and cruel axes. Again, when the whole earth rocks under their feet and towns tumble with the shock or doubtfully threaten to fall, what wonder that mortal men abase themselves and make over to the gods in things here on earth high prerogatives and marvellous powers, sufficient to govern all things?

To proceed, copper and gold and iron were discovered and at the same time weighty silver and the substance of lead, when fire had burnt up vast forests on the great hills, either by a discharge of heaven's lightning, or else because men waging with one another a forest war had carried fire among the enemy in order to strike terror, or because drawn on by the goodness of the soil they would wish to clear rich fields and bring the country into pasture, or else to destroy wild beasts and enrich themselves with the booty; for hunting with the pitfall and with fire came into use before the practice of enclosing the lawn with toils and stirring it with dogs. Whatever the fact is, from whatever cause the heat of flame had swallowed up the forests with a frightful crackling from their very roots and had thoroughly baked the earth with fire, there would run from the boiling veins and collect into the hollows of the ground a stream of silver and gold, as well as of copper and lead. And when they saw these afterwards cool into lumps and glitter on the earth with a brilliant gleam, they would lift them up, attracted by the bright and polished lustre, and they would see them to be moulded in a shape the same as the outline of the cavities in which each lay. Then it would strike them that these might be melted by heat and cast in any form or shape soever, and might by hammering out be brought to tapering points of any degree of sharpness and fineness, so as to furnish them with tools and enable them to cut the forests and hew timber and plane smooth the planks, and also to drill and pierce and bore. And they would set about these works just as much with silver and gold at first as with the overpowering strength of stout copper, but in vain, since their force would fail and give way and not be able like copper to stand the severe strain. At that time copper was in higher esteem and gold would lie neglected on account of its uselessness, with its dull blunted edge; now copper lies neglected, gold has mounted up to the highest place of honour. Thus time as it goes round changes the seasons of things. That which was in esteem falls at length into utter disrepute; and then another thing mounts up and issues out of its degraded state and every day is more and more coveted and blossoms forth high in honour when discovered and is in marvellous repute with men.

And now, Memmius, it is easy for you to find out by yourself in what way the nature of iron was discovered. Arms of old were hands, nails and teeth and stones and boughs broken off from the forests, and flame and fire, as soon as they had become known. Afterwards the force of iron and copper was discovered; and the use of copper was known before that of iron, as its nature is easier to work and it is found in greater quantity. With copper they would labour the soil of the earth, with copper stir up the billows of war and deal about wide-gaping wounds and seize cattle and lands; for everything defenceless and unarmed would readily yield to them with arms in hand. Then by slow steps the sword of iron gained ground and the make of the copper sickle became a byword; and with iron they began to plough through the earth's soil, and the struggles of wavering war were rendered equal. And the custom of mounting in arms on the back of a horse and guiding him with reins and showing prowess with the right hand is older than that of tempting the risks of war in a two-horsed chariot; and yoking a pair of horses is older than yoking four or mounting in arms scythed chariots. Next the Poeni taught the Lucan kine with towered body, hideous of aspect, with snake-like hand, to endure the wounds of war and to disorder the mighty ranks of Mars. Thus sad discord begat one thing after another, to affright nations of men under arms, and every day made some addition to the terrors of war.

They made trial of bulls too in the service of war and essayed to send savage boars against the enemy. And some sent before them valorous lions with armed trainers and courageous keepers to guide them and to hold them in chains; but in vain, since heated with promiscuous slaughter they would disorder in their rage the troops without distinction, shaking all about the frightful crests upon their heads; and the horsemen were not able to calm the breasts of the horses scared by the roaring and turn them with their bridle upon the enemy. The lionesses with a spring would throw their enraged bodies on all sides and would attack in the face those who met them, and others, off their guard, they would tear down from behind and twining round them would bring them to the ground overpowered by the wound, fastening on them with firm bite and with hooked claws. The bulls would toss their own friends and trample them under foot, and gore with their horns the flanks and bellies of the horses underneath and turn up the earth with threatening front. The boars too would rend their friends with powerful tusks, in their rage dyeing with their blood the weapons broken in them, dyeing with their blood, I say, the weapons broken in their own bodies; and would put to promiscuous rout horse and foot; for the tame beasts would try to avoid by shying to the side the cruel push of the tusk, or would rear up and paw the winds, all in vain, since you might see them tumbled down with their tendons severed and straw the ground in their heavy fall. Those whom they believed before to have been sufficiently broken in at home, they would see lash themselves into fury in the heat of action from wounds, shouting, flight, panic, uproar; and they could not rally any portion of them; for all the different kinds of wild beasts would fly all abroad; just as now the Lucan kine when cruelly mangled by the steel fly often all abroad, after inflicting on their friends many cruel deaths. But men chose thus to act not so much in any hope of victory, as from a wish to give the enemy something to rue at the cost of their own lives, when they mistrusted their numbers and were in want of arms.

A garment tied on the body was in use before a dress of woven stuff. Woven stuff comes after iron, because the loom is fitted with iron; and in no other way can such finely polished things be made, as heddles and spindles, shuttles and ringing yarn beams. And nature impelled men to work up the wool before womankind—for the male sex in general far excels the other in skill and is much more ingenious—until the rugged countrymen so upbraided them with it that they were glad to give it over into the hands of the women and take their share in supporting hard toil, and in such hard work hardened body and hands.

But nature, parent of things, was herself the first model of sowing and first gave rise to grafting, since berries and acorns dropping from the trees would put forth in due season swarms of young shoots underneath; and hence also came the fashion of inserting grafts in their stocks and planting in the ground young saplings over the fields. Next they would try another and yet another kind of tillage for their loved piece of land and would see the earth better the wild fruits through genial fostering and kindly cultivation. And they would force the forests to recede every day higher and higher up the hillside and yield the ground below to tilth, in order to have on the uplands and plains meadows, tanks, runnels, cornfields and glad vineyards, and allow a gray-green strip of olives to run between and mark the divisions, spreading itself over hillocks and valleys and plains; just as you now see richly dight with varied beauty all the ground which they lay out and plant with rows of sweet fruit trees and enclose all round with plantations of other goodly trees.

But imitating with the mouth the clear notes of birds was in use long before men were able to sing in tune smooth-running verses and give pleasure to the ear. And the whistlings of the zephyr through the hollows of reeds first taught peasants to blow into hollow stalks. Then step by step they learned sweet plaintive ditties, which the pipe pours forth pressed by the fingers of the players, heard through pathless woods and forests and lawns, through the unfrequented haunts of shepherds and abodes of unearthly calm. These things would soothe and gratify their minds when sated with food; for then all things of this kind are welcome. Often therefore, stretched in groups on the soft grass beside a stream of water under the boughs of a high tree, at no great cost they would pleasantly refresh their bodies, above all when the weather smiled and the seasons of the year painted the green grass with flowers. Then went round the jest, the tale, the peals of merry laughter; for the peasant muse was then in its glory; then frolic mirth would prompt to entwine head and shoulders with garlands plaited with flowers and leaves, and to advance in the dance out of step and move the limbs clumsily and with clumsy foot beat mother earth; which would occasion smiles and peals of merry laughter, because all these things then from their greater novelty and strangeness were in high repute. And the wakeful found a solace for want to sleep in this, in drawing out a variety of notes and going through tunes and running over the reeds with curving lip; whence even at the present day watchmen observe these traditions and have lately learned to keep the proper tune; and yet for all this receive not a jot more of enjoyment than erst the rugged race of sons of earth received. For that which we have in our hands, if we have known before nothing pleasanter, pleases above all and is thought to be the best; and as a rule the later discovery of something better spoils the taste for the former things and changes the feelings in regard to all that has gone before. Thus began distaste for the acorn, thus were abandoned those sleeping places strawn with grass and enriched with leaves. The dress too of wild beasts' skin fell into neglect; though I can fancy that in those days it was found to arouse such jealousy that he who first wore it met his death by an ambuscade, and after all it was torn in pieces among them and, drenched in blood, was utterly destroyed and could not be turned to any use. In those times, therefore, skins, now gold and purple plague men's lives with cares and wear them out with war. And in this, methinks, the greater blame rests with us; for cold would torture the naked sons of earth without their skins; but us it harms not in the least to do without a robe of purple, spangled with gold and large figures, if only we have a dress of the people to protect us. Mankind therefore ever toils vainly and to no purpose and wastes life in groundless cares, because, sure enough, they have not learnt what is the true end of getting and up to what point genuine pleasure goes on increasing: this by slow degrees has carried life out into the deep sea and stirred up from their lowest depths the mighty billows of war.

But those watchful guardians, sun and moon, traversing with their light all round the great revolving sphere of heaven, taught men that the seasons of the year came round and that the system was carried on after a fixed plan and fixed order.

Already they would pass their life fenced about with strong towers, and the land, portioned out and marked off by boundaries, be tilled; the sea would be filled with ships scudding under sail; towns have auxiliaries and allies as stipulated by treaty, when poets began to consign the deeds of men to verse; and letters had been invented not long before. For this reason our age cannot look back to what has gone before, save where reason points out any traces.

Ships and tillage, walls, laws, arms, roads, dress and all suchlike things, all the prizes, all the elegancies too of life without exception, poems, pictures and the chiselling fine-wrought statues, all these things practice, together with the acquired knowledge of the untiring mind, taught men by slow degrees as they advanced on the way step by step. Thus time by degrees brings each several thing forth before men's eyes and reason raises it up into the borders of light; for things must be brought to light one after the other and in due order in the different arts, until these have reached their highest point of development.

Book Six

In days of yore Athens of famous name imparted corn-producing crops to suffering mankind, and modelled life anew and passed laws; and first too bestowed sweet solaces of existence, when she gave birth to a man who showed himself gifted with such a genius and poured forth all knowledge of old from his truth-telling mouth; whose glory, even now that he is dead, on account of his godlike discoveries confirmed by length of time, is spread among men and reaches high as heaven. For when he saw that the things which their needs imperiously demand for subsistence had all without exception been already provided for men, and that life, so far as was possible, was placed on a sure footing, that men were great in affluence of riches and honours and glory and swelled with pride in the high reputation of their children, and yet that none of them at home for all that had a heart the less disquieted, and that it in despite of the mind plagued life without any respite and was constrained to rave with distressful complainings, he then perceived that the vessel itself did cause the corruption and that by its corruption all the things that came into it and were gathered together from abroad, however, salutary, were spoilt within it; partly because he saw it to be leaky and full of holes so that it could never by any means be filled full; partly because he perceived that it befouled, so to say, with a nauseous flavour everything within it, which it had taken in. He therefore cleansed men's breasts with truth-telling precepts and fixed a limit to lust and fear and explained what was the chief good which we all strive to reach, and pointed out the road by which, along a narrow track, we might arrive at in a straightforward course; he showed too what evils existed in mortal affairs throughout, rising up and manifoldly flying about by a natural—call it chance or force, because nature had so brought it about; and from what gates you must sally

161

out duly to encounter each; and he proved that mankind most-ly without cause arouse in their breast the melancholy tum-bling billows of cares. For even as children are flurried and dread all things in the thick darkness, thus we in the daylight fear at times things not a whit more to be dreaded than what children shudder at in the dark and fancy sure to be. This ter-ror therefore and darkness of mind must be dispelled not by the rays of the sun and glittering shafts of day, but by the aspect and law of nature. Wherefore the more readily I will go on in my verses to complete the web of my design.

And since I have shown that the quarters of ether are mor-tal and that heaven is formed of a body that had a birth, and since of all the things which go on and must go on in it, I have unravelled most, hear further what remains to be told; since once for all [I have willed] to mount the illustrious chariot [of the muses, and ascending to heaven to explain the true law of winds and storms, which men foolishly lay to the charge of the gods, telling how, when they are angry, they raise fierce tem-pests; and when there is a lull in the fury] of the winds, how that anger is appeased, how the omens which have been are again changed, when their fury has thus been appeased; [I have willed at the same time] to explain all the other things which mortals observe to go on upon earth and in heaven, when often they are in anxious suspense of mind, and which abase their souls with fear of the gods and weigh and press them down to earth, because ignorance of the causes constrains them to submit things to the empire of the gods and to make over to them the kingdom. For they who have been rightly taught that the gods lead a life without care, if nevertheless they wonder on what plan all things can be carried on, above all in regard to those things which are seen overhead in the ethereal borders, are borne back again into their old religious scruples and take unto themselves hard taskmasters, whom they, poor wretches, believe to be almighty, not knowing what can, what cannot be, in short on what principle each thing has its powers defined, its deep-set boundary mark; and therefore they are led all the farther astray by blind reason. Now unless you drive from your mind with loathing all those things, and banish far from you all belief in things degrading to the gods and inconsistent with their peace, then often will the holy deities of the gods, having their majesty lessened by you, do you hurt; not that the supreme power of the gods can be so outraged, that in their wrath they shall resolve to exact sharp vengeance, but because you will fancy to yourself that they, though they enjoy quiet and calm peace, do roll great billows of wrath; nor will you approach the sanctuaries of the gods with a calm breast nor will you be able with tranquil peace of mind to take in those idols which are carried from their holy body into the minds of men, as heralds of their divine form. And what kind of life follows after this may be conceived. But in order that most veracious reason may drive it far away from us, though much has already gone forth from me, much, however, still remains and has to be embellished in smooth-polished verses; the law and aspect of heaven has to be apprehended; storms and bright lightnings, what they do and from what cause they are borne along; all this has to be sung, that you may not mark out the heaven into quarters and be startled and distracted on seeing from which of them the volant fire has come or to which of the two halves it has betaken itself, in what way it has gained an entrance within walled places, and how after lording it with tyrant sway, it has gotten itself out from these. Do thou, deft muse Calliope, solace of men and joy of gods, point out the course before me as I race to the white boundary line of the final goal, that under thy guidance I may win the crown with signal applause.

In the first place, the blue of heaven is shaken with thunder because the ethereal clouds clash together as they fly aloft when the winds combat from opposite quarters. For no sound ever comes from a cloudless part of heaven, but wheresoever the clouds are gathered in a denser mass, from that part with greater frequency comes a clap with a loud growl. Again, clouds cannot be either of so dense a body as stones and timbers, nor again so fine as mists and flying bodies of smoke; for then they must either fall, borne down by their dead weight like stones, or like smoke they would be unable to keep together and hold within frozen snows and hail showers. They also give forth a sound over the levels of the wide-stretching upper world, just as at times a canvas awning stretched over large theatres makes a creaking noise, when it tosses about among the poles and beams; sometimes too, rent by the boisterous gales, it madly howls and closely imitates the crackling noise of pieces of paper: this kind of noise too you may notice in thunder, when the winds whirl about with their blows and buffet through the air either a hanging cloth or flying bits of

paper. For sometimes too the clouds cannot meet front to front
in direct collision, but must rather move from the flank and
so with contrary motions graze leisurely along each other's
bodies; whence comes that dry sound which brushes the ears
and is long drawn out, until they have made their way out of
their confined positions.

In this way also all things appear to quake often from the
shock of heavy thunder, and the mighty walls of the far-
stretching ether seem in an instant to have been riven and to
have sprung asunder; when a storm of violent wind has suddenly gathered and worked itself into the clouds and, there
shut in, with its whirling eddy ever more and more on all sides
forces the cloud to become hollow with a thick surrounding
crust of body; afterwards, when its force and impetuous onset
has split it, then the cloud thus rent gives forth a crash with a
hideous hurtling noise. And no wonder, when a small bladder
filled with air often emits a great sound if suddenly burst.

It can also be explained how the winds, when they blow
through the clouds, make noises: we see branching and rough
clouds often borne along in many ways; thus, you are to know,
when the blasts of the northwest blow through a dense forest,
the leaves give forth a rustling and the boughs a crashing.
Sometimes too the force of the strong wind when aroused
rends the cloud, breaking through it by an assault right in
front: what a blast of wind can do there is shown by facts
plain to sense, when here on earth where it is gentler it yet
twists out tall trees and tears them up from their deepest roots.
There are also waves among the clouds and they give a kind
of roar as they break heavily; just as in deep rivers and on the
great sea when the surf breaks. Sometimes too when the burning force of thunder has fallen out of one cloud into another, if
haply the latter contains much moisture when it has taken the
fire into it, it drowns it at once with a loud noise; just so iron
glowing hot from the fiery furnaces sometimes hisses, when we
have plunged it quickly into cold water. Again, if the cloud
which receives the fire is drier, it is set on fire in an instant
and burns with a loud noise; just as if a flame should range
over the laurel-covered hills through a whirlwind and burn
them up with its impetuous assault; and there is not anything
that burns in the crackling flame with a more startling sound
than the Delphic laurel of Phoebus. Then often too, much
crushing of ice and tumbling in of hail make a noise in the

great clouds on high; for when the wind packs them together into a confined space, the mountains of storm clouds congealed and mixed with hail break up.

It lightens too when the clouds have struck out by their collision many seeds of fire; just as if a stone were to strike another stone or a piece of iron; for then too light bursts out and fire scatters about bright sparks. But we hear the thunder with our ears after the eyes see the flash of lightning, because things always travel more slowly to the ears than those which excite vision travel to the eyes. This you may perceive from the following instance as well: when you see a man at a distance cutting with a double-edged axe a large tree, you perceive the stroke before the blow carries the sound to the ear: thus we see lightning too before we hear the thunder, which is discharged at the same time as the fire from the same cause, being born indeed from the same collision.

Also in the following manner clouds dye places with winged light and the storm flashes out with a rapid quivering movement. When the wind has made its way into a cloud and, whirling about in it, has, as I have shown above, made the cloud hollow with a dense crust, it becomes hot by its own velocity: thus you see all things thoroughly heated and fired by motion; nay, a leaden ball in whirling through a long course even melts. When therefore this wind now on fire has rent the black cloud, it scatters abroad at once seeds of fire pressed out by force, so to speak, and these produce the throbbing flashes of flame; then follows a sound which strikes on the ears more slowly than the things which travel to our eyes strike on them. This, you are to know, takes place when the clouds are dense and at the same time piled up on high one above the other in marvellous accumulation; that you be not led into error, because we see how great their breadth is below, rather than to how great a height they are piled up. Observe, at a time when the winds shall carry clouds like to mountains with a slanting course through the air, or when you shall see them piled on the sides of great mountains one on the top of the other and pressing down from above perfectly at rest, the winds being buried on all sides: you will then be able to observe their great masses and to see caverns, as it were, built of hanging rocks; and when a storm has gathered and the winds have filled these, they chafe with a loud roaring shut up in the clouds, and bluster in their dens after the fashion of wild beasts: now from this point, now from that, the winds send their growlings through the clouds, and seeking a way out, whirl about and roll together seeds of fire out of the clouds and then gather many into a mass and make flame rotate in the hollow furnaces within, until they have burst the cloud and shone forth in forked flashes.

From this cause again yon golden colour of clear bright fire flies down with velocity to the earth: the clouds must themselves have very many seeds of fire; for when they are without any moisture, they are mostly of a brilliant flame colour. Moreover, they must take in many from the sun's light, so that with good cause they are ruddy and shed forth fires. When therefore the wind has driven, thrust, squeezed together and collected into one spot these clouds, they press out and shed forth seeds which cause the colours of flame to flash out. It also lightens when the clouds of heaven are rarefied as well. For when the wind lightly unravels and breaks them up as they move, those seeds which produce the lightning must fall perforce; and then it lightens without a hideous startling noise and without any uproar.

Well, to proceed, what kind of nature thunderbolts possess is shown by their strokes and the traces of their heat which have burnt themselves into things and the marks which exhale the noxious vapours of sulphur: all these are signs of fire, not of wind or rain. Again, they often set on fire even the roofs of houses and with swift flame rule resistless within the house. This fire subtle above all fires nature, you are to know, forms of minute and lightly moving bodies, and it is such as nothing whatever can withstand. The mighty thunderbolt passes through the walls of houses, like a shout and voices, passes through stones, through brass, and in a moment of time melts brass and gold; and causes wine too in an instant to disappear, while the vessels are untouched, because, sure enough, its heat on reaching it readily loosens and rarefies all the earthen material of the vessel on every side and, forcing a way within, lightly separates and disperses the first-beginnings of the wine. This the sun's heat would be unable to accomplish in an age, though beating on it incessantly with its quivering heat: so much more nimble and overpowering is this other force.

And now in what way these are begotten and are formed with a force so resistless as to be able with their stroke to burst asunder towers, throw down houses, wrench away beams and rafters, and cast down and burn up the monuments of men, to strike men dead, prostrate cattle far and near—by what force they can do all this and the like, I will make clear and will not longer detain you with mere professions.

Thunderbolts we must suppose to be begotten out of dense clouds piled up high; for they are never sent forth at all when the sky is clear or when the clouds are of a slight density. That this is so beyond all question is proved by facts evident to sense: clouds at such times form so dense a mass over the whole sky that we might imagine all its darkness had abandoned Acheron throughout and filled up the great vaults of heaven: in such numbers, mid the frightful night of storm clouds that has gathered, do faces of black horror hang over us on high; what time the storm begins to forge its thunderbolts. Very often again a black storm cloud too out at sea, like a stream of pitch sent down from heaven, falls in such wise upon the waters heavily charged with darkness afar off and draws down a black tempest big with lightnings and storms, itself so fraught above all the rest with fires and winds that even on land men shudder and seek shelter. Thus then we must suppose that the storm above our head reaches high up; for the clouds would never bury the earth in such thick darkness unless they were built up high, heap upon heap, the sunlight totally disappearing; nor could the clouds when they descend drown it with so great a rain as to make rivers overflow and put fields under water, if they were not piled high up in the sky. In this case then, all things are filled with winds and fire; therefore thunderings and lightnings go on all about. For I have shown above that hollow clouds have very many seeds of heat, and they must also take many in from the sun's rays and their heat. On this account, when the same wind which happens to collect them into any one place has forced out many seeds of heat and has mixed itself up with that fire, then the eddy of wind forces a way in and whirls about in the straitened room and points the thunderbolt in the fiery furnaces within; for it is kindled in two ways at once: it is heated by its own velocity and from the contact of fire. After that, when the force of the wind has been thoroughly heated and the impetuous power of the fire has entered in, then the thunderbolt, fully forged, as it were, suddenly rends the cloud, and their heat, put in motion, is carried on, traversing all places with flashing lights. Close upon it follows so heavy a clap that it seems to crush down from above the quarters of heaven which have all at once sprung asunder. Then a trembling violently seizes the earth and rumblings run through high heaven; for the whole body of the storm then without exception quakes with the shock and loud roarings are aroused. After this shock follows so heavy and copious a rain that the whole ether seems to be turning into rain and then to be tumbling down and returning to a deluge: so great a flood of it is discharged by the bursting of the cloud and the storm of wind, when the sound flies forth from the burning stroke. At times too the force of the wind aroused from without falls on a cloud hot with a fully forged thunderbolt; and when it has burst it, forthwith there falls down yon fiery eddying whirl which in our native speech we call a thunderbolt. The same takes place on every other side towards which the force in question has borne down. Sometimes too the power of the wind, though discharged without fire, yet catches fire in the course of its long travel, and while it is passing on, it loses on the way some large bodies which cannot like the rest get through the air; and gathers together out of the air itself and carries along with it other bodies of very small size which mix with it and produce fire by their flight; very much in the same way as a leaden ball becomes hot during its course, when it loses many bodies of cold and has taken up fire in the air. Sometimes too the force of the blow itself strikes out fire, when the force of wind discharged in a cold state without fire has struck, because sure enough, when it has smitten with a powerful stroke, the elements of heat are able to stream together out of the wind itself and at the same time out of the thing which then encounters the stroke. Thus, when we strike a stone with iron, fire flies out; and none the less, because the force of the iron is cold, do its seeds of fiery brightness meet together upon the stroke. Therefore in the same way too a thing ought to be set on fire by the thunderbolt, if it has happened to be in a state suited to receive and susceptible of the flames. At the same time, the might of the wind cannot lightly be thought to be absolutely and decidedly cold, seeing that it is discharged with such force from above; but if it is not already set on fire during its course, it yet arrives in a warm state with heat mixed up in it.

But the velocity of thunderbolts is great and their stroke

powerful, and they run through their course with a rapid descent, because their force when aroused first in all cases collects itself in the clouds and gathers itself up for a great effort at starting; then when the cloud is no longer able to hold the increased moving power, their force is pressed out and therefore flies with a marvellous moving power, like to that with which missiles are carried when discharged from powerful engines. Then too the thunderbolt consists of small and smooth elements, and such a nature it is not easy for anything to withstand; for it flies between and passes in through the porous passages; therefore it is not checked and delayed by many collisions, and for this reason it glides and flies on with a swift moving power. Next, all weights without exception naturally pressing downward, when, moreover, a blow is added, the velocity is doubled and yon moving power becomes so intense that the thunderbolt dashes aside more impetuously and swiftly whatever gets in its way and tries to hinder it, and pursues its journey. Then too, as it advances with a long-continued moving power, it must again and again receive new velocity, which ever increases as it goes on and augments its powerful might and gives vigour to its stroke; for it forces all the seeds of the thunder to be borne right onward to one spot, so to speak, throwing them all together, as on they roll, into that single line. Perhaps too, as it goes on, it attracts certain bodies out of the air itself, and these by their blows kindle apace its velocity. It passes too through things without injuring them, and leaves many things quite whole after it has gone through, because the clear bright fire flies through by the pores. And it breaks to pieces many things, when the first bodies of the thunderbolt have fallen exactly on the first bodies of these things, at the points where they are intertwined and held together. Again, it easily melts brass and fuses gold in an instant, because its force is formed of bodies minutely small and of smooth elements, which easily make their way in, and when they are in, in a moment break up all the knots and untie the bonds of union. And more especially in autumn, the mansion of heaven, studded with glittering stars, and the whole earth are shaken on all sides, and also when the flowery season of spring discloses itself. For during the cold, fires are wanting, and winds fail during the heat, and the clouds then are not of so dense a body. When therefore the seasons of heaven are between the two extremes, the dif-

ferent causes of thunder and lightning all combine; for the
very crosscurrent of the year mixes up cold and heat, both
of which a cloud needs for forging thunderbolts; so that there
is great discord in things and the air, raving with fires and
winds, heaves in mighty disorder. The first part of heat and
the last of cold is the springtime; therefore unlike things must
battle with one another and be turbulent when mixed together.
And when the last heat mixed with the first cold rolls on its
course, a time which goes by the name of autumn, then too
fierce winters are in conflict with summers. Therefore these
seasons are to be called the cross seas of the year; and it is not
wonderful that in that season thunderbolts are most frequent,
and troublous storms are stirred up in heaven; since both
sides then engage in the troublous medley of dubious war, the
one armed with flames, the other with winds and water commingled.

This is the way to see into the true nature of the thunderbolt and to understand by what force it produces each effect,
and not the turning over the scrolls of Tyrrhene charms and
vainly searching for tokens of the hidden will of the gods, in
order to know from what quarter the volant fire has come or to
which of the two halves it has betaken itself, in what way it
has gained an entrance within walled places, and how after
lording it with tyrant sway it has gotten itself out from these;
also what harm the thunderstroke from heaven can do. But if
Jupiter and other gods shake with an appalling crash the glittering quarters of heaven, and hurl their fire whither each is so
minded, why strike they not those, whoever they be, who have
recked not of committing some abominable sin and make them
give forth the flames of lightning from breast pierced through
and through, a sharp lesson to men? And why rather is he
whose conscience is burdened with no foul offence, innocent
though he be, wrapped and enveloped in the flames, in a
moment caught up by the whirlwind and fire of heaven? Why
too aim they at solitary spots and spend their labour in vain?
Or are they then practising their arms and strengthening their
sinews? And why do they suffer the father's bolt to be blunted
on the earth? Why does he allow it himself, and not spare it for
his enemies? Why again, when heaven is unclouded on all
sides, does Jupiter never hurl a bolt on the earth or send
abroad his claps? Or does he, so soon as clouds have spread
under, then go down in person into them, that from them

he may aim the strokes of his bolt near at hand? Ay and for what reason does he hurl into the sea? Of what has he to impeach its waters and liquid mass and floating fields? Again, if he wills us to avoid the thunderstroke, why fears he to let us see it discharged? Or if he wills to crush us off our guard with his fire, why thunders he from that side, to enable us to shun it? Why stirs he up beforehand darkness and roarings and rumblings? And how can you believe that he hurls at many points at the same time? Or would you venture to maintain that it never has happened that more than one stroke was made at one time? Nay, often and often it has happened and must happen that, even as it rains and showers fall in many different quarters, so many thunderings go on at one time. Once more, why does he dash down the holy sanctuaries of the gods and his own gorgeous seats with the destroying thunderbolt, and break the fine-wrought idols of the gods, and spoil his own images of their glory by an overbearing wound? And why does he mostly aim at lofty spots, and why do we see most traces of his fire on the mountaintops?

To proceed, it is easy from these facts to understand in what way those things, which the Greeks from their nature have named presters, come down from above into the sea. For sometimes a pillar, so to speak, is let down from heaven and descends into the sea, and round about it the surges boil, roused by heavy blasts of winds; and all ships caught in that turmoil are dashed about and brought into extreme danger. This takes place when at times the force of the wind aroused cannot burst the cloud which it essays to burst, but weighs it down, so that it is like a pillar let down from heaven into the sea, yet gradually, just as if a thing were thrust down from above and stretched out to the level of the waters by the fist and push of the arm; and when the force of the wind has rent this cloud, it bursts out from it into the sea and occasions a marvellous boiling in the waters; for the whirling eddy descends and brings down together with it yon cloud of limber body; and as soon as it has forced it down full-charged as it is to the levels of the sea, the eddy in a moment plunges itself entire into the water, and stirs up the whole sea with a prodigious noise and forces it to boil. Sometimes too the eddy of wind wraps itself up in clouds and gathers out of the air seeds of cloud and imitates in a sort the prester let down from heaven. When this prester has let itself down to the land and has burst, it belches forth a whirlwind and storm of enormous violence; but as it seldom takes place at all and as mountains cannot but obstruct it on land, it is seen more frequently on the sea with its wide prospect and unobstructed horizon.

Clouds are formed, when in this upper space of heaven many bodies flying about have in some one instant met together, of a rougher sort, such as are able, though they have got the very slightest holds of each other, to catch together and be held in union. These bodies first cause small clouds to form; and these next catch together and collect into masses and increase by joining with each other and are carried on by the winds continually until a fierce storm has gathered. The nearer too the tops of a mountain in each case are to heaven, the more constantly at this elevation they smoke with the thick darkness of a swarthy cloud, because, as soon as clouds form, before the eyes can see them, thin as they are, the winds carry and bring them together to the highest summits of a mountain; and then at last when they have gathered in a greater mass, being now dense, they are able to make themselves visible and at the same time they are seen to rise up from the very top of the mountain into the ether: the very fact of the case and our sensations, when we climb high mountains, prove that the regions which stretch up on high are windy. Again, clothes hung up on the shore, when they drink in the clinging moisture, prove that nature takes up many bodies over the whole sea as well. This makes it still more plain that many bodies may likewise rise up out of the salt-heaving sea to add to the bulk of clouds; for the two liquids are near akin in their nature. Again, we see mists and steam rise out of all rivers and at the same time from the earth as well; and they, forced out like a breath from these parts, are then carried upwards and overcast heaven with their darkness and make up clouds on high as they gradually come together; for the heat of starry ether at the same time presses down too on them and by condensing, as it were, weaves a web of clouds below the blue. Sometimes there come here into heaven from without those bodies which form clouds and the flying storm rack; for I have shown that their number passes numbering and that the sum of the deep is infinite; and I have proved with what velocity bodies fly and how in a moment of time they are wont to pass through space unspeakable. It is not therefore strange that a tempest and darkness often in a short time cover over with such great storm clouds seas and lands, as they hang down upon them overhead, since on all sides through all the cavities of ether and, as it were, through the vents of the great world around, the power of going out and coming in is accorded to the elements.

Now mark and I will explain in what way the rainy moisture is formed in the clouds above and then is sent down and falls to the earth in the shape of rain. And first I will prove that many seeds of water rise up together with the clouds themselves out of all things and that both the clouds and the water which is in the clouds thus increase together; just as our body increases together with the blood, as well as the sweat and all the moisture which is in the frame. The clouds likewise imbibe much sea water as well, like hanging fleeces of wool, when the winds carry them over the great sea. In like manner moisture is taken up out of all rivers into the clouds; and when the seeds of waters, full many in number, in many ways have met in them, augmented from all sides, then the close-packed clouds endeavour to discharge their moisture from two causes: the force of the wind drives them together, and likewise the very abundance of the rain clouds, when a greater mass than usual has been brought together, pushed down, presses from above and forces the rain to stream out. Again, when the clouds are also rarefied by the winds, or are dispersed, being smitten at the same time by the heat of the sun, they discharge a rainy moisture and trickle down, just as wax over a hot fire melts away and turns fast into liquid. But a violent rain follows, when the clouds are violently pressed upon by both causes, by their own accumulated weight and by the impetuous assault of the wind. And rains are wont to hold out and to last long, when many seeds of waters are stirred to action, and clouds upon clouds and rack upon rack, welling forth from all quarters round about, are borne along, and when the reeking earth steams moisture back again from its whole surface. When in such a case the sun has shone with his rays amid the murky tempest right opposite the dripping rain clouds, then the colour of the rainbow shows itself among the black clouds.

As to the other things which grow by themselves and are formed by themselves, as well as the things which are formed within the clouds, all, without exception all—snow, winds, hail and cold hoarfrosts and the great force of ice, the great congealing power of waters, and the stop which everywhere curbs running rivers—it is yet most easy to find out and apprehend in mind how all these things take place and in what way they are formed, when you have fully understood the properties assigned to elements.

Now mark and learn what the law of earthquakes is. And first of all take for granted that the earth below us as well as above is filled in all parts with windy caverns and bears within its bosom many lakes and many chasms, cliffs and craggy rocks; and you must suppose that many rivers hidden beneath the crust of the earth roll on with violence waves and submerged stones; for the very nature of the case requires it to be throughout like to itself. With such things then attached and placed below, the earth quakes above from the shock of great falling masses, when underneath time has undermined vast caverns; whole mountains indeed fall in, and in an instant from the mighty shock tremblings spread themselves far and wide from that centre. And with good cause, since buildings beside a road tremble throughout when shaken by a wagon of not such very great weight; and they rock no less when any sharp pebble on the road jolts up the iron tires of the wheels on both sides. Sometimes too, when an enormous mass of soil through age rolls down from the land into great and extensive pools of water, the earth rocks and sways with the undulation of the water; just as a vessel at times cannot rest, until the liquid within has ceased to sway about in unsteady undulations.

Again, when the wind gathering itself together in the hollow places underground bears down on one point and, pushing on, presses with great violence the deep caverns, the earth leans over on the side to which the headlong violence of the wind presses. Then all buildings which are above ground—and ever the more, the more they tower up towards heaven—lean over and bulge out, yielding in the same direction, and the timbers, wrenched from their supports, hang over, ready to give way. And yet men shrink from believing that a time of destruction and ruin awaits the nature of the great world, though they see so great a mass of earth hang ready to fall! And if the winds did not abate their blowing, no force could rein things in or hold them up on their road to destruction. As it is, because by turns they do abate and then increase in violence, and, so to speak, rally and return to the charge, and then are defeated and retire, for this reason the earth oftener threatens to fall than really falls: it leans over and then sways back again, and after tumbling forward, recovers in equal poise its fixed position. For this reason the whole house rocks, the top more than the middle, the middle than the bottom, the bottom in a very, very slight degree.

The same great quaking likewise arises from this cause, when on a sudden the wind and some enormous force of air, gathering either from without or within the earth, have flung themselves into the hollows of the earth, and there chafe at first with much uproar among the great caverns and are carried on with a whirling motion, and when their force afterwards, stirred and lashed into fury, bursts abroad and at the same moment cleaves the deep earth and opens up a great yawning chasm. This fell out in Syrian Sidon and took place at Aegium in the Peloponnese, two towns which an outbreak of wind of this sort and the ensuing earthquake threw down. And many walled places besides fell down by great commotions on land and many towns sank down engulfed in the sea together with their burghers. And if they do not break out, still the impetuous fury of the air and the fierce violence of the wind spread over the numerous passages of the earth like a shivering fit and thereby cause a trembling; just as cold, when it has pierced into our frames to the very marrow, sets them ashivering in spite of themselves, forcing them to shake and move. Men are therefore disturbed by a two-edged terror throughout their cities; they fear the roofs above their heads, they dread lest the nature of the earth in a moment break up her caverns underneath and, rent asunder, display her own wide-gaping maw and, wildly tumbled together, seek to fill it up with her own ruins. Let them then fancy as much as they please that heaven and earth shall be incorruptible and consigned to an everlasting exemption from decay; and yet sometimes the very present force of danger applies on some side or other this goad of fear among others, that the earth shall in an instant be withdrawn from under their feet and carried down into the pit, and that the sum of things shall utterly give way and follow after and a jumbled wreck of world ensue.

First of all they wonder that nature does not increase the bulk of the sea, when there is so great a flow of water into it, when all rivers from all quarters fall into it. Add to these passing rains and flying storms, which bespatter every sea and moisten every land; add its own springs; yet all these compared with the sum of the sea will be like an addition of bulk hardly amounting to a single drop; it is therefore the less wonderful that the great sea does not increase. Again, the sun absorbs a great deal with his heat: we see him with his burning rays thoroughly dry clothes dripping with wet: but we know seas to be many in number and to stretch over a wide surface. Therefore, however small the portion of moisture which the sun draws off the surface from any one spot, it will yet in so vast an expanse take largely from its waters. Then again, the winds too may withdraw a great deal of moisture as they sweep over the surface, since we very often see the roads dried by the winds in a single night and the soft mud form into hard crusts. Again, I have shown that the clouds take off much moisture too imbibed from the great surface of the sea and scatter it about over the whole earth, when it rains on land and the winds carry on the clouds. Lastly, since the earth is of a porous body and is in contact with the sea, girding its shores all round, just as water comes from the earth into the sea, in the same way it must ooze into the land out of the salt sea; for the salt is strained off and the matter of liquid streams back again to the source and all flows together to the riverheads, and then passes anew over the lands in a fresh current, where a channel, once scooped out, has carried down the waters with liquid foot.

And now I will explain why it is that fires breathe forth at times through the gorges of Mount Etna with such hurricane-like fury; for with a destroying force of no ordinary kind, the flame-storm gathered itself up and, lording it over the lands of the Sicilians, drew on itself the gaze of neighbouring nations, when, seeing all the quarters of heaven smoke and sparkle, men were filled in heart with awe-struck apprehension, not knowing what strange change nature was travailing to work.

In these matters you must look far and deep and make a wide survey in all directions, in order to bear in mind that the sum of things is unfathomable and to perceive how very small, how inconceivably minute a fraction of the whole sum one heaven is, not so large a fraction of it as one man is of the whole earth. If you should clearly comprehend, clearly see this point well put, you would cease to wonder at many things. Does anyone among us wonder if he has gotten into his frame a fever that has broken out with burning heat, or into his body the pains of any other disease? The foot suddenly swells, sharp pain often seizes the teeth, or else attacks the eyes; the holy fire breaks out, and creeping over the body, burns whatever part it has seized upon, and spreads over the frame, because sure enough, there are seeds of many things, and this earth and heaven bring to us evil enough to allow of a measureless amount of disease springing up. In this way then we must suppose that all things are supplied out of the infinite to the whole heaven and earth in quantity sufficient to allow the earth in a moment to be shaken and stirred, and a rapid hurricane to scour over sea and land, the fire of Etna to overflow, the heaven to be in flames; for that too is seen and the heavenly quarters are on fire; and rain storms gather in a heavier mass, when the seeds of water have haply come together for such an end. "Ay but the stormy rage of the conflagration is too, too gigantic." Yes and so any river you like is greatest to him who has never before seen any greater, and thus a tree and a man seem gigantic, and in the case of all things of all kinds, the greatest a man has seen he fancies to be gigantic, though yet all things, with heaven and earth and sea included, are nothing to the whole sum of the universal sum.

And now at last I will explain in what ways yon flame roused to fury in a moment blazes forth from the huge furnaces of Etna. And first the nature of the whole mountain is hollow underneath, underpropped throughout with caverns of basalt rocks. Furthermore, in all caves are wind and air; for wind is produced when the air has been stirred and put in motion. When this air has been thoroughly heated and, raging about, has imparted its heat to all the rocks round, wherever it comes in contact with them, and to the earth, and has struck out from them fire burning with swift flames, it rises up and then forces itself out on high, straight through the gorges; and so carries its heat far and scatters far its ashes and rolls on smoke of a thick, pitchy blackness and flings out at the same time stones of prodigious weight; leaving no doubt that this is the stormy force of air. Again, the sea to a great extent breaks its waves and sucks back its surf at the roots of that mountain. Caverns reach from this sea as far as the deep gorges of the mountain below. Through these you must admit [that air mixed up with water passes; and] the nature of the case compels [this air to enter in from that] open sea and pass right within and then go out in blasts and so lift up flame and throw out stones and raise clouds of sand; for on the summit are craters, as they name them in their own language; what we call gorges and mouths.

There are things too, not a few, for which it is not sufficient to assign one cause; you must give several, one of which at the same time is the real cause. For instance, should you see the lifeless body of a man lying at some distance, it would be natural to mention all the different causes of death, in order that the one real cause of that man's death be mentioned among them. Thus you may be able to prove that he has not died by steel or cold or from disease or haply from poison; yet we know that it is something of this kind which has befallen him; and so in many other cases we may make the same remark.

The Nile rises in summer and overflows the plains, that one sole river throughout the whole land of Egypt. It waters Egypt often in the middle of the hot season, either because in summer there are north winds opposite its mouths, which at that time of year go by the name of etesian winds. Blowing up the river, they retard it, and driving the waters backwards, fill its channel full and force the river to stand still; for beyond a doubt these blasts which start from the icy constellations of the pole are carried right up the stream. That river comes from the south out of the heat-fraught country, rising far up from the central region of day among races of men black in their sun-baked complexion. It is quite possible too that the great accumulation of sand may bar up the mouths right across against the descending currents, when the sea, stirred up by the winds, throws up the sand within the channel; whereby the outlet of the river is rendered less free and the current of the waters at the same time less rapid in its downward flow. It may be also that the rains are more frequent at its source in that season, because the etesian blasts of the north winds drive all the clouds together into those parts at that time. And, you are to know, when they have been driven on to the central region of day and have gathered together, then the clouds, jammed close against the high mountains, are massed together and violently compressed. Perhaps too it gets its increase high up from the lofty mountains of the Ethiopians, when the all-surveying sun with his thawing rays constrains the white snows to descend into the plains.

Now mark, and I will make clear to you what kind of na-

ture the several Avernian places and lakes possess. First of all,
as to the name Avernian, by which they are called, it has
been given to them from their real nature, because they are
noxious to all birds; for when they have arrived in flight just
opposite those spots, they forget to row with their wings, they
drop their sails and fall, with soft neck outstretched, headlong
to the earth, if so be that the nature of the ground admit of
that, or into the water, if so be that a lake of Avernus spreads
below. There is such a spot at Cumae, where the mountains
are charged with acrid sulphur, and smoke enriched with hot
springs. Such a spot there also is within the Athenian walls,
on the very summit of the citadel, beside the temple of boun-
tiful Tritonian Pallas, which croaking crows never come near
on the wing; no, not when the high altars smoke with offerings: so constantly they fly, not before the sharp wrath of
Pallas for the sake of yon vigil kept, as the poets of the Greeks
have sung, but the nature of the place suffices by its own
proper power. In Syria too, as well as a spot, we are told, is found
to exist of such a sort that as soon as ever even four-footed
beasts have entered in, its mere natural power forces them to
fall down heavily, just as if they were felled in a moment as
sacrifices to the manes gods. Now all these things go on by a
natural law, and it is quite plain whence spring the causes
from which they are produced; that the gate of Orcus be not
haply believed to exist in such spots; and next we imagine
that the manes gods from beneath do haply draw souls down
from them to the borders of Acheron; as wing-footed stags are
supposed often by their scent to draw out from their holes the
savage serpent tribes. How widely opposed to true reason this
is, now learn; for now I essay to tell of the real fact.

First of all I say, as I have often said before, that in the
earth are elements of things of every kind: many, which serve
for food, helpful to life; and many whose property it is to cause
diseases and hasten death. And we have shown before that
one thing is more adapted to one, another thing to another
living creature for the purposes of life, because of their natures
and their textures and their primary elements being all unlike
the one to the other. Many which are noxious pass through
the ears, many make their way too through the nostrils, dangerous and harsh when they come in contact; and not a few
are to be shunned by the touch, and not a few to be avoided
by the sight, and others are nauseous in taste.

Again, you may see how many things are for man of a viru-
lently noxious sensation and are nauseous and oppressive; to
certain trees, for instance, has been given so very oppressive a
shade that they often cause headaches when a man has lain
down under them extended on the grass. There is a tree too
on the great hills of Helicon which has the property of killing
a man by the noisome scent of its flower. All these things,
you are to know, rise up out of the earth, because it contains
many seeds of many things in many ways mixed up together
and gives them out in a state of separation. Again, when a
newly extinguished night light encounters the nostrils with its
acrid stench, it sends to sleep then and there a man who from
disease is subject to falling down and foaming at the mouth.
A woman is put to sleep by oppressive castor and falls back in
her seat, and her gay work drops out of her soft hands, if she
has smelt it at the time when she has her monthly discharges.
And many things besides relax through all the frame the fainting limbs and shake the soul in its seats within. Then too if
you linger long in the hot baths when you are somewhat full
and do bathe, how liable you are to tumble down in a fit while
seated in the midst of the hot water! Again, how readily do
the oppressive power and fumes of charcoal make their way
into the brain, if we have not first taken water! But when
burning with more than usual force it has filled the chambers
of a house, then the fumes of the virulent substance act like a
murderous blow. See you not too that even within the earth
sulphur is generated and asphalt forms incrustations of a noisome stench? See you not, when they are following up the
veins of silver and gold and searching with the pick quite into
the bowels of the earth, what stenches Scaptensula exhales
from below? Then what mischief do gold mines exhale! To
what state do they reduce men's faces and what a complexion
they produce! Know you not by sight or hearsay how they
commonly perish in a short time and how all vital power
fails those whom the hard compulsion of necessity confines in
such an employment? All such exhalations then the earth
steams forth and breathes out into the open air and light of
heaven.

Thus too the Avernian spots must send up some power
deadly to birds, which rises up from the earth into the air so
as to poison a certain portion of the atmosphere; in such a
way that a bird, as soon as ever it is borne on its wings into

it, is then attacked by the unseen poison and so palsied that it tumbles plump down on the spot where this exhalation has its course. And when it falls into it, then the same power of that exhalation robs all its limbs of the remnants of life: first of all it causes a sort of dizziness; but afterwards, when the birds have tumbled into the very springs of the poison, then life too has to be vomited forth, because all round rises up large store of mischievous matter.

Sometimes too this power and exhalation of Avernus dispels whatever air lies between the birds and earth, so that almost a void is left there. And when the birds have arrived in their flight just opposite this spot, at once the buoyant force of their pinions is crippled and rendered vain and all the sustaining efforts of their wings are lost on both sides. So when they are unable to buoy themselves up and lean upon their wings, nature, you know, compels them by their weight to tumble down to earth, and lying stark through what is now almost a void, they disperse their souls through all the openings of their body. . . . Again, during summer the water in wells becomes colder, because the earth is rarefied by heat and rapidly sends out into the air whatever seeds of heat it happens to have. The more then the earth is drained of heat, the colder becomes the water which is hidden in the earth. Again, when all the earth is compressed by cold and contracts and, so to say, congeals, it then, you are to know, while it contracts, presses out into the wells whatever heat it contains itself.

At the fane of Hammon there is said to be a fountain which is cold in the daylight and hot in the nighttime. This fountain men marvel at exceedingly and suppose that it suddenly becomes hot by the influence of the fierce sun below the earth, when night has covered the earth with awful darkness. But this is far, far removed from true reason. Why, when the sun, though in contact with the uncovered body of the water, has not been able to make it hot on its upper side, though his light above possesses such great heat, how can he below the earth, which is of so dense a body, boil the water and glut it with heat? Above all, when he can scarcely with his burning rays force his heat through the walls of houses. What then is the cause? This sure enough: the earth is more porous and warmer round the fountain than the rest of the earth, and there are many seeds of fire near the body of water. For this reason, when night has buried the earth in its dewy shadows,

the earth at once becomes quite cold and contracts: in this
way, just as if it were squeezed by the hand, it forces out into
the fountain whatever seeds of fire it has; and these make the
water hot to the touch and taste. Next, when the sun has risen
and with his rays has loosened the earth and has rarefied it as
his heat waxes stronger, the first-beginnings of fire return back
to their ancient seats and all the heat of the water withdraws
into the earth: for this reason the fountain becomes cold in
the daylight. Again, the liquid of water is played upon by the
sun's rays and in the light is rarefied by his throbbing heat;
and therefore it gives up whatever seeds of fire it has; just as
it often parts with the frost which it holds in itself, and thaws
the ice and loosens its bonds.

There is also a cold fountain of such a nature that tow often
when held over it imbibes fire forthwith and emits flame; a
pine torch in like manner is lighted and shines among the
waters, in whatever direction it swims under the impulse of
the winds. Because, sure enough, there are in the water very
many seeds of heat, and from the earth itself at the bottom
must rise up bodies of fire throughout the whole fountain and
at the same time pass abroad in exhalations and go forth into
the air, not in such numbers, however, that the fountain can
become hot, for these reasons a force compels those seeds to
burst out through the water and disperse abroad and to unite
when they have mounted up. In the sea at Aradus is a fountain of this kind, which wells up with fresh water and keeps
off the salt waters all round it; and in many other quarters
the sea affords a seasonable help in need to thirsting sailors,
vomiting forth fresh waters amid the salt. In this way then
those seeds may burst forth through that fountain and well out
into the tow. And when they meet together in it or cohere in
the body of the pine torch, they at once readily take fire, because the tow and pinewood contain in them likewise many
seeds of latent fire. See you not too that, when you bring a
newly extinguished wick near night lamps, it catches light before it has touched the flame; and the same with the pinewood? And many things besides catch fire at some distance
touched merely by the heat, before the fire in actual contact
infects them. This therefore you must suppose to take place in
that fountain as well.

Next in order I will proceed to discuss by what law of nature it comes to pass that iron can be attracted by that stone

which the Greeks call the magnet, from the name of its native place, because it has its origin within the bounds of the country of the Magnesians. This stone men wonder at; as it often produces a chain of rings hanging down from it. Thus you may see sometimes five and more suspended in succession and tossing about in the light airs, one always hanging down from one and attached to its lower side, and each in turn one from the other experiencing the binding power of the stone: with such a continued current its force flies through all.

In things of this kind many points must be established before you can assign the true law of the thing in question, and it must be approached by a very circuitous road; wherefore all the more I call for an attentive ear and mind.

In the first place, from all things whatsoever which we see there must incessantly stream and be discharged and scattered abroad such bodies as strike the eyes and provoke vision. Smells too incessantly stream from certain things; as does cold from rivers, heat from the sun, spray from the waves of the sea, that eater into walls near the shore. Various sounds too cease not to stream through the air. Then a moist salt flavour often comes into the mouth, when we are moving about beside the sea; and when we look on at the mixing of a decoction of wormwood, its bitterness affects us. In such a constant stream from all these things the several qualities of things are carried and are transmitted in all directions round, and no delay, no respite in the flow is ever granted, since we constantly have feeling, and may at any time see, smell and hear the sound of anything.

And now I will state once again how rare a body all things have, a question made clear in the first part of my poem also. Although the knowledge of this is of importance in regard to many things, above all in regard to this very question which I am going to discuss, at the very outset it is necessary to establish that nothing comes under sense save body mixed with void. For instance, in caves rocks overhead sweat with moisture and trickle down in oozing drops. Sweat too oozes out from our whole body; the beard grows and hairs over all our limbs and frame. Food is distributed through all the veins, gives increase and nourishment to the very extremities and nails. We feel too cold and heat pass through brass, we feel them pass through gold and silver, when we hold full cups. Again, voices fly through the stone partitions of houses; smell passes through and cold and the heat of fire, which is wont, ay, to pierce even the strength of iron, where the Gaulish cuirass girds the body round. And storms that have gathered in earth and heaven withdraw respectively to heaven and earth and there do work their wills; and along with them the influence of disease, when it makes its way in from without; since there is nothing at all that is not of a rare texture of body.

Furthermore, all bodies whatever which are discharged from things are not qualified to excite the same sensations nor are adapted for all things alike. The sun, for instance, bakes and dries up the earth, but thaws ice, and forces the snows piled up high on the high hills to melt away beneath his rays; wax again turns to liquid when placed within reach of his heat. Fire also melts brass and fuses gold, but shrivels up and draws together hides and flesh. The liquid of water after fire hardens steel, but softens hides and flesh hardened by heat. The wild olive delights the bearded she-goats as much as if the flavour of ambrosia and nectar in truth streamed from it; but nothing that puts forth leaf is more bitter to man than this food. Again, a swine eschews marjoram oil and dreads all perfumes; for they are rank poison to bristly swine, though they are found at times to give us, as it were, fresh life. But on the other ha~ ₁, though mire is to us the nastiest filth, it is found to be so welcome to swine that they wallow in it all over, with a craving not to be satisfied.

There is still one point left which it seems proper to mention, before I come to speak of the matter in hand. Since many pores are assigned to various things, they must possess natures differing the one from the other and must have each its own nature, its own direction: thus there are in living creatures various senses, each of which takes into it in its own peculiar way its own special object; for we see that sounds pass into one thing, taste from different flavours into another thing, smells into another. Again, one thing is seen to stream through stones and another thing to pass through woods, another through gold, and another still to go out through silver and brass; for form is seen to stream through this passage, heat through that, and one thing is seen to pass through by the same way more quickly than other things. The nature of the passages, you are to know, compels it so to be, varying in manifold wise, as we have shown a little above, owing to the unlike natures and textures of things.

Therefore, now that these points have all been established and arranged for us as premises ready to our hand, for what remains, the law will easily be explained out of them, and the whole cause be laid open which attracts the strength of iron. First of all, there must stream from this stone very many seeds or a current, if you will, which dispels with blows all the air which lies between the stone and iron. When this space is emptied and much room left void between, forthwith the first-beginnings of iron fall headlong forward into the void in one mass, and in consequence the ring itself follows and then goes on with its whole body. And nothing has its primal elements more intricately entangled or coheres in closer connexion than the nature of stubborn iron and its coldness that makes you shiver. Therefore what I say is the less strange, that from among such elements as these, bodies cannot gather in large numbers out of the iron and be carried into the void without the whole ring following. This it does do, and follows on until it has quite reached the stone and fastened on it with unseen bonds of connexion. The same thing takes place in all directions: on whatever side a void is formed, whether athwart or from above, the first bodies next it are at once carried on into the void; for they are set in motion by blows from another source and cannot by their own free act rise up into the air. Moreover (to render it more feasible, this thing also is helped on by external aid and motion), as soon as the air in front of the ring has been made rarer and the space more empty and void, it follows at once that all the air which lies behind carries and pushes it on, as it were, at its back. For the air which lies around them always beats on things; but at such a time as this it is able to push on the iron, because on one side a space is void and receives the iron into it. This air of which I am speaking to you makes its way with much subtlety through the frequent pores of the iron to its minute parts and then thrusts and pushes it on, as the wind a ship and its sails. Again, all things must have air in their body, since they are of a rare body and air surrounds and is in contact with all things. This air therefore, which is in the inmost recesses of the iron, is ever stirred in restless motion and therefore beats the ring without a doubt and stirs it within, you know: the ring is carried in the direction in which it has once plunged forward, and into the void part towards which it has made its start.

Sometimes too it happens that the nature of iron is repelled from this stone, being in the habit of flying from and following it in turns. I have seen Samothracian iron rings even jump up, and at the same time filings of iron rave within brass basins, when this magnet stone had been placed under: such a strong desire the iron seems to have to fly from the stone. So great a disturbance is raised by the interposition of the brass because, sure enough, when the current of the brass has first seized on and taken possession of the open passages of the iron, the current of the stone comes after and finds all things full in the iron and has no opening to swim through as before. It is forced therefore to dash against and beat with its wave the iron texture; by which means it repels from it and sets in motion through the brass that which without the brass it often draws to itself. And forbear herein to wonder that the current from this stone is not able to set in motion other things as well as iron: some of these stand still by the power of their own weight; for instance, gold; and others, because they are of so rare a body that the current flies through them uninterrupted, cannot in any case be set in motion; to which class wood is found to belong. When therefore the nature of iron lying between the two has received into it certain first bodies of brass, then do the magnet stones set it in motion with their stream.

And yet these cases are not so much at variance with other things, that i have only a scanty store of similar instances to relate of things mutually fitted one for the other and for nothing else. Stones, for instance, you see are cemented by mortar alone; wood is united with wood so firmly by bulls' glue only, that the veins of boards often gape in cracks before the binding power of the glue can be brought to loosen its hold. Vineborn juices venture to mix with streams of water, though heavy pitch and light oil cannot. Again, the purple dye of the shellfish so unites with the body of wool alone that it cannot in any case be severed, not were you to take pains to undo what is done with Neptune's wave, not if the whole sea were willed to wash it out with all its waters. Then too is there not one thing only that fastens gold to gold, and is not brass soldered to brass by tin? And how many other cases of the kind might one find! What then? You have no need whatever of such long circuitous roads, nor is it worth my while to spend so much pains on this, but it is better briefly to comprise many things in few words: things whose textures have such a mutual correspondence that cavities fit solids, the cavities of the first the solids of the second, the cavities of the second the solids of the first, form the closest union. Again, some things may be fastened together and held in union with hooks and eyes, as it were; and this seems rather to be the case with this stone and iron.

And now I will explain what the law of diseases is and from what causes the force of disease may suddenly gather itself up and bring death-dealing destruction on the race of man and the troops of brute beasts. And first I have shown above that there are seeds of many things helpful to our life; and on the other hand, many must fly about conducing to disease and death. When these by chance have happened to gather together and have disordered the atmosphere, the air becomes distempered. And all that force of disease and that pestilence come either from without down through the atmosphere in the shape of clouds and mists, or else do gather themselves up and rise out of the earth when, soaked with wet, it has contracted a taint, being beaten upon by unseasonable rains and suns. See you not too that all who come to a place far away from country and home are affected by the strangeness of climate and water, because there are wide differences in such things? For what a difference may we suppose between the climate of the Briton and that of Egypt where the pole of heaven slants askew, and again between that in Pontus and that of Gades, and so on to the races of men black with sun-baked complexion? Now as we see these four climates under the four opposite winds and quarters of heaven all differing from each other, so also the complexions and faces of the men are seen to differ widely and diseases varying in kind are found to seize upon the different races. There is the elephant disease which is generated beside the streams of Nile in the midst of Egypt and nowhere else. In Attica the feet are attacked and the eyes in Achaean lands. And so different places are hurtful to different parts and members: the variations of air occasion that. Therefore when an atmosphere which happens to put itself in motion unsuited to us and a hurtful air begin to advance, they creep slowly on in the shape of mist and cloud and disorder everything in their line of advance and compel all to change; and when they have at length reached our atmosphere, they corrupt it too and make it like to themselves and unsuited to us. This new destroying power and pestilence therefore either fall upon the waters or else sink deep into the corn crops or

other food of man and provender of beast; or else their force
remains suspended within the atmosphere, and when we inhale from it mixed airs, we must absorb at the same time into
our body those things as well. In like manner pestilence often
falls on kine also and a distemper too on the silly sheep. And
it makes no difference whether we travel to places unfavour-
able to us and change the atmosphere which wraps us round,
or whether nature without our choice brings to us an atmosphere unsuited to us or something to the use of which we have
not been accustomed, and which is able to attack us on its first
arrival.

Such a form of disease and a death-fraught miasm erst within the borders of Cecrops defiled the whole land with dead,
and dispeopled the streets, drained the town of burghers. Rising first and starting from the inmost corners of Egypt, after
traversing much air and many floating fields, the plague
brooded at last over the whole people of Pandion; and then
they were handed over in troops to disease and death. First of
all they would have the head seized with burning heat and
both eyes bloodshot with a glare diffused over; the livid throat
within would exude blood and the passage of the voice be
clogged and choked with ulcers, and the mind's interpreter
the tongue, drip with gore, quite enfeebled with sufferings,
heavy in movement, rough to touch. Next when the force of
disease, passing down the throat, had filled the breast and had
streamed together even into the sad heart of the sufferers, then
would all the barriers of life give way. The breath would pour
out at the mouth a noisome stench, even as the stench of rotting carcases thrown out unburied. And then the powers of
the entire mind, the whole body would sink utterly, now on
the very threshold of death. And a bitter, bitter despondency
was the constant attendant on insufferable ills and complaining mingled with moaning. An ever-recurring hiccup often the
night and day through, forcing on continual spasms in sinews
and limbs, would break men quite, forwearying those forspent
before. And yet in none could you perceive the skin on the
surface of the body burn with any great heat, but the body
would rather offer to the hand a lukewarm sensation and at
the same time be red all over with ulcers burnt into it, so to
speak, like unto the holy fire as it spreads over the frame. The
inward parts of the men, however, would burn to the very
bones; a flame would burn within the stomach as within fur-

naces. Nothing was light and thin enough to apply to the relief of the body of anyone; ever wind and cold alone. Many would plunge their limbs, burning with disease, into the cool rivers, throwing their body naked into the water. Many tumbled headforemost deep down into the wells, meeting the water straight with mouth wide agape. Parching thirst with a craving not to be appeased, drenching their bodies, would make an abundant draught no better than the smallest drop. No respite was there of ill: their bodies would lie quite spent. The healing art would mutter low in voiceless fear, as again and again they rolled about their eyeballs wide open, burning with disease, never visited by sleep. And many symptoms of death besides would then be given, the mind disordered in sorrow and fear, the clouded brow, the fierce delirious expression, the ears too troubled and filled with ringings, the breathing quick or else strangely loud and slow-recurring, and the sweat glistening wet over the neck, the spittle in thin small flakes, tinged with a saffron colour, salt, scarce forced up the rough throat by coughing. Then tendons of the hands ceased not to contract, the limbs to shiver, a coldness to mount with slow, sure pace from the feet upwards. Then at their very last moments they had nostrils pinched, the tip of the nose sharp, eyes deep-sunk, temples hollow, the skin cold and hard, on the grim mouth a grin, the brow tense and swollen; and not long after their limbs would be stretched stiff in death: about the eighth day of bright sunlight or else on the ninth return of his lamp they would yield up life. And if any of them at that time had shunned the doom of death, yet in after time consumption and death would await him from noisome ulcers and the black discharge of the bowels, or else a quantity of purulent blood accompanied by headache would often pass out by the gorged nostrils: into these the whole strength and substance of the man would stream. Then too if anyone had escaped the acrid discharge of noisome blood, the disease would yet pass into his sinews and joints and onward even into the sexual organs of the body; and some from excessive dread of the gates of death would live bereaved of these parts by the knife; and some though without hands and feet would continue in life, and some would lose their eyes: with such force had the fear of death come upon them. And some were seized with such loss of memory that they quite forgot everything else and did not know themselves. And though bodies lay in heaps above bodies unburied on the ground, yet would the race of birds and beasts either scour far away, to escape the acrid stench, or where anyone had tasted, it drooped in near-following death. Though hardly at all in those days would any bird appear, or the sullen breeds of wild beasts quit the forests. Many would droop with disease and die; above all, faithful dogs would lie stretched in all the streets and yield up breath with a struggle; for the power of disease would wrench life from their frame. Funerals lonely, unattended, would be hurried on with emulous haste. And no sure and universal method of cure was found; for that which had given to one man the power to inhale the vital air and to gaze on the quarters of heaven would be destruction to others and would bring on death. But in such times this was what was deplorable and above all eminently heart-rending: when a man saw himself enmeshed by the disease, as though he were doomed to death, losing all spirit, he would lie with sorrow-stricken heart, and with his thoughts turned on death would surrender his life then and there. Ay, for at no time did they cease to catch from one another the infection of the devouring plague, like to woolly flocks and horned herds. And this above all heaped death on death: whenever any refused to attend their own sick, killing neglect soon after would punish them for their too great love of life and fear of death by a foul and evil death, abandoned in turn, forlorn of help. But they who had stayed by them would perish by infection and the labour which shame would then compel them to undergo and the sick man's accents of affection mingled with those of complaining: this kind of death the most virtuous would meet. . . . and different bodies on different piles, struggling as they did to bury the multitude of their dead: then spent with tears and grief they would go home; and in great part they would take to their bed from sorrow. And none could be found whom at so fearful a time neither disease nor death nor mourning assailed.

Then too every shepherd and herdsman, ay and sturdy guider of the bent plough, sickened; and their bodies would lie huddled together in the corners of a hut, delivered over to death by poverty and disease. Sometimes you might see lifeless bodies of parents above their lifeless children, and then the reverse of this, children giving up life above their mothers and fathers. And in no small measure that affliction streamed from the land into the town, brought thither by the sickening crowd of peasants meeting plague-stricken from every side. They would fill all places and buildings: wherefore all the more the heat would [destroy them and] thus close-packed death would pile them up in heaps. Many bodies drawn forth by thirst and tumbled out along the street would lie extended by the fountains of water, the breath of life cut off from their too great delight in water; and over all the open places of the people and the streets you might see many limbs drooping with their half-lifeless body, foul with stench and covered with rags, perish away from filth of body, with nothing but skin on their bones, now nearly buried in noisome sores and dirt. All the holy sanctuaries of the gods too death had filled with lifeless bodies, and all the temples of the heavenly powers in all parts stood burdened with carcases: all which places the wardens had thronged with guests. For now no longer the worship of the gods or their divinities were greatly regarded: so overmastering was the present affliction. Nor did those rites of sepulture continue in force in the city, with which that pious folk had always been wont to be buried; for the whole of it was in dismay and confusion, and each man would sorrowfully bury as the present moment allowed. And the sudden pressure and poverty prompted to many frightful acts; thus with a loud uproar they would place their own kinsfolk upon the funeral piles of others, and apply torches, quarrelling often with much bloodshed sooner than abandon the bodies.

RECENT WASHINGTON SQUARE PRESS EDITIONS

THE GREAT AMERICAN THINKERS SERIES

Original critical works devoted to one man who represents a particular movement. General editors are Thomas S. Knight and Arthur W. Brown.

JONATHAN EDWARDS, by Alfred Owen Aldridge, Ph.D., Professor of English and Director of the Program of Comparative Literature, University of Maryland. W 881 (60¢)

JOHN WOOLMAN, by Edwin H. Cady, Ph.D., Rudy Professor of English, University of Indiana. W 882 (60¢)

THOMAS JEFFERSON, by Stuart Gerry Brown, Ph.D., Maxwell Professor of American Civilization, Syracuse University. W 876 (60¢)

JOHN C. CALHOUN, by Richard N. Current, Ph.D., Professor of History, University of Wisconsin. W 877 (60¢)

GEORGE BANCROFT, by Russel B. Nye, Ph.D., Professor of English, Michigan State University. W 879 (60¢)

CHAUNCEY WRIGHT, by Edward H. Madden, Ph.D., Professor of Philosophy, State University of New York at Buffalo. W 878 (60¢)

THORSTEIN VEBLEN, by Douglas Dowd, Ph.D., Professor of Economics, Cornell University. W 880 (60¢)

THE GREAT HISTORIES SERIES

Classics of world history selected and edited by outstanding modern scholars. The series editor is H. R. Trevor-Roper.

HERODOTUS, edited by W. G. Forrest, Fellow of Wadham College, Oxford University. W 1100 (90¢)

THUCYDIDES, edited by P. A. Brunt, Fellow of Oriel College, Oxford University. W 1101 (90¢)

TACITUS, edited by Hugh Lloyd-Jones, Regius Professor of Greek, Oxford University. W 1104 (90¢)

GUICCIARDINI, edited by J. R. Hale, Fellow of Jesus College, Oxford University. W 1106 (90¢)

VOLTAIRE, edited by J. H. Brumfitt, Senior Lecturer in French, St. Andrews University. W 1107 (90¢)

GIBBON, edited by H. R. Trevor-Roper, Regius Professor of Modern History, Oxford University. W 1108 (90¢)

HENRY ADAMS, edited by E. N. Saveth, Professor of History, The New School. W 1109 (90¢)

• • • • • • • • • • • • • • • •

You may order these titles by sending retail price, plus 10¢ per book for postage and handling, to: Mail Service Department, Washington Square Press, Inc., 1 West 39th Street, New York 18, N. Y. Please enclose check or money order—do not send cash. WSP-1(E)

GREAT SHORT STORIES

Now available in well-edited anthologies and offered in handsome, durable paperback editions at bargain prices.